LUCK
Doesn't Happen
BY CHANCE

By
Claire Doyle-Beland

P.O. Box 754
Huntsville, AR 72740
WWW.OZARKMT.COM

For permission, or serialization, condensation, adaptions, or for our catalog of other publications, write to: Ozark Mountain Publishing P.O. Box 332 West Fork, AR 72774 Attn: Permission Department.

Library of Congress Cataloging-in-Publication Data
Doyle-Beland, Claire 1936 -
   Luck Doesn't Happen By Chance / by Claire Doyle-Beland
   Using Astrology and Numerology to find your lucky cycles.

   1. Astrology.   2. Numerology.   3. Gambling.   4. Games.
I. Doyle-Beland, Claire, 1936- II. Astrology/Numerology III. Title

Library of Congress Catalog Card Number: 99-070704

ISBN: 1-886940-05-3

Cover Design: Karen Cannon
Book Set in: Times New Roman, Chancery
Book Design: Tom Cannon

Published By

P.O. Box 754
Huntsville, AR 72774
WWW.OZARKMT.COM

Printed in the United States of America

Table of Contents

DEDICATION

I would like to dedicate this book to:

My mother, the most giving person I know, who taught me good values and has always supported me in all my endeavors.

My two lovely daughters, Linda and Michelle, of whom I'm very proud. They are my reason for being and persevering.

My wonderful sons-in-law, Marc and Dan, who are the sons I never had, and always there to help me in every way.

My four beautiful grandchildren; Megan, Kyle, Janelle and Meric, who are a constant source of joy.

I love you all very dearly.

A special thank you to my brother Michael, who was an enormous help to me in putting this book together. Love you!

Claire Doyle-Beland

CHAPTER
1

The principles of numerology and astrology are a part of the natural laws governing humanity, the planets and all creation. These sciences do not contradict religious beliefs, as they provide strong evidence for a "DIVINE DESIGN".

Through the mysterious laws of vibration, we have learned how the single numbers, 1 through 9, can be used to determine the character of those born under them. The calculations of the ancient Hindus, Egyptians, Hebrews and Chaldeans, are as valid today as they were thousands of years ago. Modern scientists are still amazed at their accuracy.

A forcible illustration from the Book of the Wisdom of Solomon, in which Solomon states: "For God himself gave me an unerring knowledge of the things that are, to know the constitution of the world, the beginning and the end and middle of times, the alterations of the solstices, the changes of seasons and the position of the planets, the nature of living creatures and the thoughts of men, all things that are either secret or manifest I learned, for He that is the artificer of all things taught me this wisdom."

In this book I will reveal lucky numbers, lucky days and fortunate cycles for each sign. This information is based on numerology and astrology, which I have studied for 25 years, because I knew these sciences contained many of the answers I was seeking. Luck was one of the things that always intrigued me.

Was it all really due to chance? I didn't believe it was, and I was determined to find some of the answers. I was convinced that like everything else in this life, on this earth, and in the universe, luck was part of the Divine Plan and Design of things.

There are so many mysteries, and so much we do not know yet, so I won't pretend to have all the answers. However, after extensive reading and studying, I have concluded that one of the most important ingredients for luck is timing, knowing when to be in the right place at the right time. I discovered this because I have always enjoyed gambling. I believe that we all have the gambling instinct within us, which drives us to take chances in the hope that we will experience the thrill of being a winner. I think we would be hard-pressed to find many people who do not at least purchase a lottery ticket now and then.

I was never lucky at gambling, and in fact, I was so unlucky compared to my two gambling pals, that they nicknamed me "Lucky" as a joke. Out of desperation, about five years ago, I started keeping a record of the dates and times I gambled and the amount of my winnings, which were few and far between back then. I was hoping this would reveal some kind of pattern, but I never dreamed that one day these records would be so valuable in proving the accuracy of my findings.

A few years ago, I took an early retirement. Since I had a lot of time on my hands, I started delving into my numerology and astrology books, which I had not been able to do for many years, due to the demanding work I had been involved in. One day, all the pieces of the puzzle fell into place. By combining ancient scientific principles with modern technology, I devised a chart of lucky numbers, lucky days, lucky hours and fortunate cycles, which were mainly based on my date of birth. I compared this chart to the records I had been keeping, and I was astounded to discover that 99% of my winnings involved my lucky numbers and lucky periods.

During my years of record keeping, I had also kept track of the larger winnings of my two gambling pals, and after checking this information with their charts, I found the same amazing results. This is also how I found out why my two friends had been luckier than me. We usually did our gambling on the same days of the week, which turned out to be more to their advantage than mine.

I have been using my luck chart for over two years, and not only am I winning more often, I am saving myself a lot of money by not gambling when the odds are not in my favor. I gave other people their own personal luck charts, and there have been countless success stories. All of them experienced increased good luck in their gambling and every-day life as well. I am truly convinced that luck doesn't happen by chance.

The Greek philosopher, Pythagoras, the father of mathematics, laid down the axiom that numbers concealed and contained the secret of the universe. Everything on earth and above the earth has its meaning, its place, position and number, in the order of things, which is the highest form of Design. Every day of the week, every hour of the day and every minute of the hour, has both its meaning and number. Do not ascribe the course of your life to "chance"; to do so is to insult your Creator.

NUMBERS FOR DAYS OF THE WEEK

SUNDAY............1 - 4   MONDAY...........2 - 7
TUESDAY..............9   WEDNESDAY........5
THURSDAY...........3   FRIDAY...................6
SATURDAY...........8

THESE NUMBERS CORRESPOND
TO THE PLANETS
AS FOLLOWS:

SUN...............1 - 4   MOON.............2 - 7
JUPITER.............3   URANUS..............4
MERCURY.........5   VENUS.................6
NEPTUNE..........7   SATURN.............8
MARS.................9

The Sun and the Moon are the only two planets that have "double numbers". The Sun and Uranus are interrelated one to another, so the number of the Sun is written as 1 - 4. The Moon is interrelated with Neptune and is written as 2 - 7.

The day of birth gives a key number that is related to the planet bearing the same number, which represents a vibration that lasts all through life. The birth date plays an important part in each person's personal luck chart, and it also determines what sign you are. The great philosopher, Ptolemy, claimed that "Judgment must be regulated by thyself, as well as by science. It is most advantageous to make choices of days and hours at a time constituted by the nativity".

BIRTH DATES ON THE CUSPS

When I first became interested in astrology, I was confused because I was born on the cusp of Aquarius and Pisces, February 19th. Some of the books showed this date as Aquarius and others as Pisces. I used to buy books for both signs, and after a while I determined I was more Aquarius than Pisces. However, it wasn't until I took my first course on astrology, that I discovered for sure I was an Aquarian. The truth is, one can be born on this date and be an Aquarian or a Piscean, it all depends on the year of birth. This applies to all persons with a birth date on any of the cusps. Over the years, I have encountered a great number of people who, like me, did not know for sure what their true sign was. This information should be included in all books of astrology to eliminate confusion, but unfortunately it is not.

To find out what sign you are, check the following pages.

Year	Aries Mar-Apr	Taurus Apr-May	Gemini May-June	Cancer June-July	Leo July-Aug	Virgo Aug-Sept
1910	22-20	21-21	22-21	22-23	24-23	24-23
1911	22-20	21-21	22-22	23-23	24-23	24-23
1912	21-19	20-20	21-21	22-22	23-23	24-22
1913	21-20	21-21	22-21	22-23	24-23	24-23
1914	21-20	21-21	22-21	22-23	24-23	24-23
1915	22-20	21-21	22-22	23-23	24-23	24-23
1916	21-19	20-20	21-21	22-22	23-23	24-22
1917	21-20	21-21	22-21	22-22	23-23	24-23
1918	21-20	21-21	22-21	22-23	24-23	24-23
1919	22-20	21-21	22-21	22-23	24-23	24-23
1920	21-19	20-20	21-21	22-22	23-22	23-22
1921	21-20	21-21	22-21	22-22	23-23	24-23
1922	21-20	21-21	22-21	22-23	24-23	24-23
1923	22-20	21-21	22-21	22-23	24-23	24-23
1924	21-19	20-20	21-21	22-22	23-22	23-22
1925	21-20	21-21	22-21	22-22	23-23	24-23
1926	21-20	21-21	22-21	22-23	24-23	24-23
1927	22-20	21-21	22-21	22-23	24-23	24-23
1928	21-19	20-20	21-21	22-22	23-22	23-22
1929	21-20	21-21	22-21	22-22	23-23	24-23
1930	21-20	21-21	22-21	22-23	24-23	24-23
1931	22-20	21-21	22-21	22-23	24-23	24-23
1932	21-19	20-20	21-21	22-22	23-22	23-22
1933	21-20	21-21	22-21	22-22	23-23	24-23
1934	21-20	21-21	22-21	22-23	24-23	24-23
1935	22-20	21-21	22-21	22-23	24-23	24-23
1936	21-19	20-20	21-21	22-22	23-22	23-22
1937	21-20	21-20	21-21	22-22	23-23	24-22
1938	21-20	21-21	22-21	22-23	24-23	24-23
1939	22-20	21-21	22-21	22-23	24-23	24-23

Libra	Scorpio	Sagittarius	Capricorn	Aquarius	Pisces
Sept-Oct	Oct-Nov	Nov-Dec	Dec-Jan	Jan-Feb	Feb-Mar
24-23	24-22	23-22	23-20	21-19	20-21
24-24	25-22	23-22	23-20	21-19	20-21
23-23	24-22	23-21	22-20	21-19	20-20
24-23	24-22	23-21	22-20	21-18	19-20
24-23	24-22	23-22	23-20	21-18	19-20
24-24	25-22	23-22	23-20	21-19	20-21
23-23	24-22	23-21	22-20	21-19	20-20
24-23	24-22	23-21	22-20	21-18	19-20
24-23	24-22	23-22	23-20	21-18	19-20
24-23	24-22	23-22	23-20	21-19	20-21
23-23	24-22	23-21	22-20	21-19	20-20
24-23	24-22	23-21	22-20	21-18	19-20
24-23	24-22	23-22	23-20	21-18	19-20
24-23	24-22	23-22	23-20	21-19	20-21
23-23	24-22	23-21	22-20	21-19	20-20
24-23	24-22	23-21	22-20	21-18	19-20
24-23	24-22	23-22	23-20	21-18	19-20
24-23	24-22	23-22	23-20	21-19	20-21
23-23	24-22	23-21	22-20	21-19	20-20
24-23	24-22	23-21	22-20	21-18	19-20
24-23	24-22	23-22	23-20	21-18	19-20
24-23	24-22	23-22	23-20	21-19	20-21
23-23	24-22	23-21	22-20	21-19	20-20
24-23	24-22	23-21	22-19	20-18	19-20
24-23	24-22	23-22	23-20	21-18	19-20
24-23	24-22	23-22	23-20	21-19	20-21
23-23	24-21	22-21	22-20	21-19	20-20
23-23	24-22	23-21	22-19	2--18	19-20
24-23	24-22	23-22	23-20	21-18	19-20
24-23	24-22	23-22	23-20	21-19	20-21

Year	Aries Mar-Apr	Taurus Apr-May	Gemini May-June	Cancer June-July	Leo July-Aug	Virgo Aug-Sept
1940	21-19	20-20	21-21	22-22	23-22	23-22
1941	21-19	20-20	21-21	22-22	23-23	24-22
1942	21-20	21-21	22-21	22-23	24-23	24-23
1943	22-20	21-21	22-21	22-23	24-23	24-23
1944	21-19	20-20	21-21	22-22	23-22	23-22
1945	21-19	20-20	21-21	22-22	23-23	24-22
1946	21-20	21-21	22-21	22-22	23-23	24-23
1947	21-20	21-21	22-21	22-23	24-23	24-23
1948	21-19	20-20	21-21	22-22	23-22	23-22
1949	21-19	20-20	21-21	22-22	23-22	23-22
1950	21-20	21-21	22-21	22-22	23-23	24-23
1951	22-20	21-21	22-21	23-23	24-23	24-23
1952	21-20	21-21	22-21	22-22	23-23	24-23
1953	21-20	21-21	22-21	22-23	24-23	24-23
1954	22-20	21-21	22-21	22-23	24-23	24-23
1955	22-20	21-21	22-22	23-23	24-23	24-23
1956	21-20	21-21	22-21	22-22	23-23	24-23
1957	21-20	21-21	22-21	22-23	24-23	24-23
1958	22-20	21-21	22-21	22-23	24-23	24-23
1959	22-20	21-21	22-22	23-23	24-23	24-23
1960	21-20	21-21	22-21	22-22	23-23	24-23
1961	21-20	21-21	22-21	22-23	24-23	24-23
1962	22-20	21-21	22-21	22-23	24-23	24-23
1963	22-20	21-21	22-22	23-23	24-23	24-23
1964	21-20	21-21	22-21	22-22	23-23	24-23
1965	21-20	21-21	22-21	22-23	24-23	24-23
1966	22-20	21-21	22-21	22-23	24-23	24-23
1967	22-20	21-21	22-21	23-23	24-23	24-23
1968	21-20	21-20	22-22	22-22	23-23	24-22
1969	21-20	21-21	22-21	22-23	24-23	24-23

Libra	Scorpio	Sagittarius	Capricorn	Aquarius	Pisces
Sept-Oct	Oct-Nov	Nov-Dec	Dec-Jan	Jan-Feb	Feb-Mar
23-23	24-21	22-21	22-20	21-19	20-20
23-23	24-22	23-21	22-19	20-18	19-20
24-23	24-22	23-21	22-20	21-18	19-20
24-23	24-22	23-22	23-20	21-19	20-21
23-23	24-21	22-21	22-20	21-19	20-20
23-23	24-22	23-21	22-19	20-18	19-20
24-23	24-22	23-21	22-20	21-18	19-20
24-23	24-22	23-22	23-20	21-18	19-20
23-23	24-21	22-21	22-20	21-19	20-20
23-23	24-22	23-21	22-19	20-18	19-20
24-23	24-22	23-21	22-20	21-18	19-20
24-23	25-23	24-22	23-20	21-19	20-21
24-23	24-22	23-21	22-21	22-19	20-20
24-23	24-22	23-22	23-20	21-18	19-20
24-23	24-22	23-22	23-20	21-19	20-21
24-24	25-23	24-22	23-20	21-19	20-21
24-23	24-22	23-21	22-21	22-19	20-20
24-23	24-22	23-22	23-20	21-18	19-20
24-23	24-22	23-22	23-20	21-19	20-21
24-24	25-23	24-22	23-20	21-19	20-21
24-23	24-22	23-21	22-21	22-19	20-20
24-23	24-22	23-22	23-20	21-18	19-20
24-23	24-22	23-22	23-20	21-19	20-21
24-24	25-23	24-22	23-20	21-19	20-21
24-23	24-22	23-21	22-21	22-19	20-20
24-23	24-22	23-22	23-20	21-18	19-20
24-23	24-22	23-22	23-20	21-19	20-21
24-24	25-22	23-22	23-20	21-19	20-21
23-23	24-22	23-21	22-20	21-19	20-20
24-23	24-22	23-22	23-20	21-18	19-20

Year	Aries Mar-Apr	Taurus Apr-May	Gemini May-June	Cancer June-July	Leo July-Aug	Virgo Aug-Sept
1970	22-20	21-21	22-21	22-23	24-23	24-23
1971	22-20	21-21	22-22	23-23	24-23	24-23
1972	21-19	20-20	21-21	22-22	23-23	24-22
1973	21-20	21-21	22-21	22-22	23-23	24-23
1974	22-20	21-21	22-21	22-23	24-23	24-23
1975	22-20	21-21	22-22	23-23	24-23	24-23
1976	21-19	20-20	21-21	22-22	23-23	24-22
1977	21-20	21-21	22-21	22-22	23-23	24-23
1978	21-20	21-21	22-21	22-23	24-23	24-23
1979	22-20	21-21	22-21	22-23	24-23	24-23
1980	21-19	20-20	21-21	22-22	23-22	23-22
1981	21-20	21-21	22-21	22-22	23-23	24-23
1982	21-20	21-21	22-21	22-23	24-23	24-23
1983	22-20	21-21	22-21	22-23	24-23	24-23
1984	21-19	20-20	21-21	22-22	23-22	23-22
1985	21-20	21-21	22-21	22-22	23-23	24-23
1986	21-20	21-21	22-21	22-23	24-23	24-23
1987	22-20	21-21	22-21	22-23	24-23	24-23
1988	21-19	20-20	21-21	22-22	23-22	23-22
1989	21-20	21-21	22-21	22-22	23-23	24-23
1990	21-20	21-21	22-21	22-23	24-23	24-23
1991	22-20	21-21	22-21	22-23	24-23	24-23
1992	21-19	20-20	21-21	22-22	23-22	23-22
1993	21-20	21-21	22-21	22-22	23-23	24-23
1994	21-20	21-21	22-21	22-23	24-23	24-23
1995	22-20	21-21	22-21	22-22	23-23	24-23
1996	21-20	20-20	21-21	22-22	23-23	23-22
1997	21-20	21-21	22-21	22-22	23-23	24-22
1998	21-20	21-21	22-21	22-23	24-23	24-23
1999	22-20	21-21	22-21	22-23	24-23	24-23

Libra	Scorpio	Sagittarius	Capricorn	Aquarius	Pisces
Sept-Oct	Oct-Nov	Nov-Dec	Dec-Jan	Jan-Feb	Feb-Mar
24-23	24-22	23-22	23-20	21-19	20-21
24-24	25-22	23-22	23-20	21-19	20-21
23-23	24-22	23-21	22-20	21-19	20-20
24-23	24-22	23-22	23-20	21-18	19-20
24-23	24-22	23-22	23-20	21-19	20-21
24-24	25-22	23-22	23-20	21-19	20-21
23-23	24-22	23-21	22-20	21-19	20-20
24-23	24-22	23-21	22-20	21-18	19-20
24-23	24-22	23-22	23-20	21-19	20-20
24-24	25-22	23-22	23-20	21-19	20-21
23-23	24-22	23-21	22-20	21-19	20-20
24-23	24-22	23-21	22-20	21-18	19-20
24-23	24-22	23-22	23-20	21-18	19-20
24-23	24-22	23-22	23-20	21-19	20-21
23-23	24-22	23-21	22-20	21-19	20-20
24-23	24-22	23-21	22-20	21-18	19-20
24-23	24-22	23-22	23-20	21-18	19-20
24-23	24-22	23-22	23-20	21-19	20-21
23-23	24-22	23-21	22-20	21-19	20-20
24-23	24-22	23-21	22-20	21-18	19-20
24-23	24-22	23-22	23-20	21-18	19-20
24-23	24-22	23-22	23-20	21-19	20-21
23-23	24-22	23-21	22-20	21-19	20-20
24-23	24-22	23-21	22-20	21-18	19-20
24-23	24-22	23-22	23-20	21-18	19-20
24-23	24-22	23-22	23-20	21-19	20-21
23-23	24-22	23-21	22-20	21-19	20-20
23-23	24-22	23-21	22-20	21-18	19-20
24-23	24-22	23-22	23-20	21-18	19-20
24-23	24-22	23-22	23-20	21-19	20-21

CHAPTER

2

PREPARING YOUR "LUCK" CALENDAR

Once you have obtained all the lucky numbers and lucky periods indicated in the section of your Sun sign, refer back to this page, and I will explain how to consolidate everything on a calendar.

Your lucky numbers, and all the dates that add up to these numbers, are lucky on any day of the week, but much more so, if they fall on any of your lucky days, especially on the lucky day assigned to these numbers.

This might sound a little confusing. You certainly do not want to be sorting out this information every day, so I will show you a method I developed for myself. You will find it very advantageous, because you will have all this important information available at a glance. I strongly suggest you use it, because if you don't, you will probably end up tucking this book away in a drawer. It certainly will not do you any good there.

Here's what to do:

On a fair sized calendar, circle all the dates mentioned in your lucky numbers. If the dates you circled fall on the day assigned to that number, put an X next to that date. Underline your three or four lucky days of the week for the whole month.

The following is an example of a monthly calendar that has been prepared, using my own birth date, February 19th, and my sun sign Aquarius.

My first lucky number is - 3 (12-21-30) - lucky day Thursday.

My second lucky number is - 1 (10-19-28) - lucky days Sunday and Monday.

My third lucky number is - 4 (13-22-31) - lucky day Saturday, which is the number assigned to my ruling planet Uranus, and also number - 8 (17-26) which is the number assigned to Saturn, the co-ruling planet of Aquarius.

NOTE: As indicated previously, the numbers 1 and 4 are assigned to the Sun and Sunday. The numbers 2 and 7 are assigned to the Moon and Monday. If your birth date is 1-10-19-28 or 4-13-22-31, these numbers are related and the lucky day is Sunday. If your birth date is 2-11-20-29 or 7-16-25, these numbers are also related, and the lucky day is Monday.

Since number - 4 - is my third lucky number and since it is also related to my birth date number - 1 -, this would indicate that number - 4 - would be especially lucky for me. I would like to point out that the records I kept for five years confirm the fact that I won much more often on days and numbers adding up to - 4 -, and I also have won more often on Sundays and Mondays.

It has been proven that there is an attraction between the numbers 1, 2, 4 and 7, which means they are interrelated. If your birth date is one of these dates, you will be fortunate with all these numbers on Sunday and Monday. Since my birth date is on the 19th, this applies to me.

On the following calendar, I have circled all the dates mentioned in my lucky numbers. I have inserted an "X" next to Monday the 13th, Sunday the 19th, and Monday the 20th, because these numbers are assigned to Sundays and Mondays. I have also inserted an "X" next to Thursday the 30th, because this number is assigned to Thursdays.

Because of my birth date, I have four lucky days, which are: Sunday, Monday, Thursday and Saturday, so I have underlined all these days.

Sunday	Monday	Tuesday	Wednesday	Thursday	Friday	Saturday
			①	②	③	④
5	6	⑦	⑧	9	⑩	⑪
⑫	x ⑬	14	15	⑯	⑰	18
x⑲	x ⑳	㉑	㉒	23	24	㉕
㉖	27	㉘	㉙	x ㉚	㉛	

CALENDAR

Looking at my calendar for this particular month, my luckiest days would be the 13th, 19th, 20th and 30th, because they are circled, underlined, and have an "X". My secondary lucky numbers would be all the dates that are both circled and underlined, such as the 2nd, 4th, 12th, 16th, 25th and 26th, and so on. Then, of course, I would also check my lucky hours chart every day.

Once you have completed your own calendar, all the days that are circled (with or without an "X"), and all the days underlined will be lucky for you that month. Days that are circled and underlined, are doubly fortunate. Days that are circled and underlined, with an "X", are triply fortunate, because you now have three lucky elements working for you. If you combine your lucky hours as well, you quadruple your chances of winning. The middle hour of the three-hour lucky period is the luckiest and most powerful. As for your lucky periods during the year, you could use a highlighter or underline them in red, or come up with a system of your own. It is important to prepare a new calendar every month, because the luckiest days and secondary lucky numbers, will vary from month to month.

If you go to the casino, a bingo, horse races, buy a ticket, or do any other form of gambling, all you have to do is glance at your calendar. Within a few minutes you can choose a day and time that is most favorable for you. As you can see, the calendar is a must. I personally fill in my calendar for the whole year. It only takes me about one hour, and I'm all set until the next year. I hope you will take this information and use it repeatedly. It really does work, and it will definitely improve your luck and quality of life.

Although the periods mentioned are lucky for games of chance, they are also your best times for all other areas of your life, such as making important decisions; looking for employment; choosing a career; interviews; a change of residence or buying a new home; making large purchases such as cars, boats, furniture; choosing a room-mate or getting married, etc. Accurate judgment is necessary for the success of any enterprise, yet by combining this with the fundamental laws of cause and effect outlined by the science of the universe, a greater measure of success may be attained. In other words, if you make use of the information I am providing you in the section of your sun sign, you will not only greatly improve your odds of winning in games of chance, but your quality of life in general.

Now, let's talk about attitude. Like everything else in life, you need a positive attitude in gambling as well. You must believe you are going to win! The more you believe it, the more often it will happen. It is easier to have a winning attitude when you are following your personal luck chart, because you know your odds of winning are greater when you are in a lucky time frame. This does not mean you will win every time you gamble, but you will win more frequently. You will also save a lot of money, by avoiding gambling during time periods less fortunate for you.

Always keep a positive attitude and consult your personal luck chart regularly. If you go to a bingo, choose an afternoon or evening that coincides with your lucky hours and lucky days. If you go to a horse race, choose one of your lucky days and play your lucky numbers. If you buy a scratch ticket or a lottery ticket, consult your luck chart. The same applies if you go to a casino. You will notice on your lucky hours chart that you have three or four lucky periods each day, which last for three hours. If you want to buy a ticket of any kind, or gamble for only one hour, choose the middle hour, which is the most powerful. For instance, in a lucky period between seven and ten o'clock, the luckiest hour would be between eight and nine o'clock.

Do not get discouraged if you don't happen to win right away. It takes a little while to get used to the idea of using your Luck Chart. Once you get into the habit, you will notice your luck steadily improving. Just keep trying and developing a winning attitude.

Before you know it, you'll be saying, "Hey! I am lucky!"

CHAPTER
3
~⁓⟨❦⟩⁓~

FORTUNATE CYCLES

The following fortunate cycles apply to everybody, regardless of birth date. At the ages of, 16, 20, 22, 26, 28, 32, 34, 38, 40, 44, 46, 50, 56, 58, 62, 64, 68, 70, 74 and 80.

These are times when things come our way, when we receive many gifts, when we win at games of chance, or when the opposite sex favors us. Your fortunate cycles last about nine months, and start about four months before your birth month to four months afterwards. For many of us, those are the years of prosperity.

This is not to say that you will not have some difficulties during those years, but some good fortune should come your way, somebody will help you, an opportunity will present itself, and chances for making money are good. To those out of work, it means that they will be able to find employment, even if it is not exactly what they would like to do. Changes made will prove profitable and business will increase. It marks a fortunate time for expanding in business, for taking long journeys, for legal affairs, or to establish yourself securely.

History records many amazing predictions about the

destiny of nations, rulers, and individuals, all based on cycles. This was the secret of the Egyptians and all past civilizations. It is up to every one of us to make use of those cycles in our affairs. Before making plans for the future, you should check to see if you are under a fortunate cycle. If so, then you can go ahead with your plans, expand, take chances, and make radical changes in your affairs.

It is hoped that with this information, you will be more successful and find greater happiness. Nothing can be more valuable than to know whether you are lucky now, or whether you must be on your guard. Realize how many times fate has been kind to you and you did not take the opportunity. When your affairs are going smoothly and success is yours, and you know that it is part of a fortunate cycle, you can time its end and thus not expect your luck to last longer than it really will. Enjoy the good things that come your way, but if fate is unkind to you, you will want to know just when luck, success, and happiness will be yours again.

IMPORTANT FACTS CONCERNING NUMBERS "4" AND "8"

In numerology, it is strongly recommended to never increase the power of the numbers "4" and "8", and their series (4-13-22-31 and 8-17-26). To do so, could bring sadness, ill-luck, or terrible blows of fate. These numbers generally attract one another, and as single numbers, they can be lucky. However, to combine these numbers, is not considered lucky.

I know for a fact, that combining number 4 and number 8 can be fatalistic, because it happened to me, and I have the documents to prove it.

I bought a new car on April (4th month) the 8th. My payments were made on the 8th of each month. My license plates consisted of three letters and the numbers "404". Two months later, on June 8th, I had my first accident, and on September 26th (2+6=8), I had a second accident. The following year, I moved from one province to another, and had to change my license plates. I was given one which included three letters and the numbers "880". On December 4th that year, I was involved in a third accident, and my car was a total wreck, so I had to buy a new one. I did not realize at the time, that this was a blessing, because I was getting away from the combination of numbers "4" and "8", which had caused me a lot of grief in many ways.

When I started to seriously study numerology, shortly after my last accident, my experience with these numbers was instrumental in reinforcing my belief in this science. I should point out that prior to these three car accidents I had been driving for thirty years, and during that period of time I was involved in only one minor accident.

When you consult your sun sign, to discover your lucky numbers, if you have a number from the "4" series and a number from the "8" series, it would definitely be wise to drop one of them. If one of these numbers is your birth date, retain that number and refrain from combining it with the opposite series of numbers.

NOTE: The above applies even more so to people born under the signs of Capricorn and Aquarius, since #8 is the number assigned to the planet Saturn, ruler of Capricorn, and #4 is the number assigned to the planet Uranus, ruler of Aquarius. (As mentioned previously in my book, I am an Aquarian).

FEAR OF NUMBER 13 UNFOUNDED

A great number of people dread the number 13, but to tell you the truth, it is not unlucky at all. In ancient times, it was regarded as a fatalistic number by many. One of the main reasons was because the Church claimed that since 13 sat down to the Last Supper, it would be unlucky if 13 were to eat together. However, if Christ had not been crucified, the Scriptures would not have been fulfilled, and Christianity would never have existed.

It is interesting to note, that the dread of number 13 has a limited geographical range. In the Indian Pantheon, there are 13 Buddhas, and Buddha, like Christ, had 12 apostles. The mystical discs which surmount Indian and Chinese pagodas, are 13 in number. Enshrined in the Temple Of Atsua in Japan, is a sacred sword with 13 objects of mystery forming its hilt. The sacred number of the Mexicans was 13, and they had 13 snake gods.

Another fascinating example is the Great Seal of the U.S.A. The face of the American Seal shows 13 stripes on the shield; 13 stars in the circle of glory; 13 branches and 13 berries in the olive branch in the eagle's right talon; and 13 arrows in the left talon. None of this is coincidental! It was decreed by law that there must be a repetition of the number 13 in the seal's composition. On the reverse side, there are 13 layers of stone in the unfinished pyramid. The legend "Annuit Coeptis" contains 13 letters, corresponding to the 13 stripes in the American flag. During the Civil War, even though the Confederacy had only eleven states, their flag had 13 stars. There are all kinds of odd correlations in American history connected to the number 13. There is nothing accidental about this. Thirteen harmonizes with the fundamental pattern in Nature.

Hopefully, all these facts will help many people get rid of their dread for number 13.

I personally believe it is a very lucky number.

CHAPTER
4

CHARACTERISTICS AND OTHER
FACTS RELATED TO
BIRTH DATES

BIRTH DATE: 1 - 10 - 19 - 28

Number -1- people are positive, ambitious, and determined in all they undertake. They often rise to positions of authority and strive to make themselves respected and looked up to. They dislike restraint, so many are self-employed, or are in jobs allowing them a lot of freedom. When they are genuinely appreciated, they will bend over backwards to please. They can be creative, inventive, and very generous. They are affectionate with those they love, and there's a special fondness for children and young people. They encourage individuality in their own children, and listen to their opinions. They love fine clothes and jewelry, and mix styles according to their own rules. Number 1 people have an inbred sense of dignity.

Their most fortunate colors are all shades of gold, yellows and browns.

Their lucky jewels are the topaz, amber and yellow diamond; also all stones of these colors. Wearing a piece of amber next to their skin is fortunate.

BIRTH DATE: 2 - 11 - 20 - 29

Number -2- people are romantic and gentle by nature. Their qualities are more on the mental plane. Their intuition is highly developed and they are psychic, though some may not realize it. They are born listeners, and your secrets are safe with them. Being peacemakers, they often find solutions to other people's problems. There's a deep devotion or involvement (in either a negative or positive sense) to the parents, especially the mother. They have a deep concern for family, friends and relatives. Being imaginative, they are often artistic. Most of them dislike taking chances, and prefer to invest their money securely. They love to travel when finances permit, but for number 2 individuals, "home is where the heart is."

Their most fortunate colors are all shades of green, white and cream. Whenever possible, they should avoid dark colors such as black or purple.

Their lucky jewels are pearls, pale green stones and moonstones. They should carry a piece of jade with them, or wear it next to their skin.

BIRTH DATE: 3 - 12 - 21 - 30

Number -3- people are great communicators, and have a certain personal charm. They have a facility with words, spoken or written. They love fun and humor, and the more self-confident they feel, the more gregarious they become. They love beautiful things and surroundings, and their welcome mat is usually well-worn by a constant stream of guests, eager to enjoy their hospitality. They are conscious of their youthful appearance, and usually go to great lengths to preserve and enhance it. Number 3 individuals are proud, independent and ambitious. They do not like restraint, so they usually end up with positions of authority, self employed, or have a lot of freedom in the work or profession they choose. They are happiest when surrounded by people.

Their most fortunate colors are shades of mauve, violet or purple. All shades of blue, crimson and rose are favorable to them.

Their lucky jewel is the amethyst, and they should always have a piece on their person or next to their flesh.

BIRTH DATE: 4 - 13 - 22 - 31

Number -4- people have a distinct character of their own, and usually have a serious approach to life. They were born to work hard, and are organized and ultimate planners. They are honest, trustworthy and creatures of habit. Not being gamblers, they prefer the prudent approach in everything. As a rule, they are more or less indifferent to the accumulation of wealth. They have excellent memories, and a great store of practical knowledge. Number 4 people are good with their hands, and have a knack for fixing things. Being sensitive and sentimental, they are usually inclined to take the part of the underdog. They are often inclined towards social reforms. Family life is their foundation, and they take their parenting responsibilities seriously.

Their most fortunate colors are half-shades or electric colors. Greys and electric blues suit them best.

Their lucky jewel is the sapphire. If possible, they should wear this stone next to their skin.

BIRTH DATE: 5 - 14 - 23

Number -5- people are very aware of what's going on in the world. Always in search of new experiences, they're curious to see what's around the next bend. They make decisions quickly, are impulsive, and often mentally high-strung. They need freedom and dislike being restricted. They love all kinds of electrical gadgets, and are clever at assembling things. Number 5   is sociable, fun loving, makes friends easily, and gets along with almost everyone. They are active, energetic and naturally keep fit. Since they like to live on the edge, they give their children the same freedom to take chances and grow. They rebound quickly from the heaviest blows of fate, with little indentation on their character.

Their most fortunate colors are white, grey and glistening materials. They can wear all shades of colors, but the light shades are best.

Their lucky jewels are the diamond and all glittering things. If possible, they should wear a diamond set in platinum or silver next to their skin.

BIRTH DATE: 6 - 15 - 24

Number -6- people are honest, fair, and keep their word. Because they are good listeners, they can be relied upon when the chips are down. They have a magnetic charm, and attract others to them. Because they cannot stand discord, they try to make everyone happy. When deeply attached, they can become devoted slaves to their loved ones. They make wonderful parents, and attract children with their warmth and patience. They love beautiful things, are quality conscious and want the best money can buy. Number 6 people are very determined in carrying out their plans, and can be very successful in a service-oriented business. They hold themselves accountable for their own work, but will also step in to help others if they sense the need.

Their most fortunate colors are all shades of blue, rose or pink. They should avoid wearing black or dark purple.

Their lucky jewels are the turquoise and the emerald. They should wear one of these next to their skin.

BIRTH DATE: 7 - 16 - 25

Number -7- people are a class act! They like to be impeccably groomed and well-dressed. They are independent and have a strong individuality. Since they are not gamblers by nature, they analyze their position, and make a move only when the odds are in their favor. "Quality time" was inspired by number 7 parents. They trust their children, and do not over-indulge them. They regard education as a lifelong pursuit. Being restless, they like change and travel. Many become good writers or painters, and are lovers of fine music. They love to read about the customs and cultures of foreign countries. In their book, material success and philanthropy go hand in hand; the good they give always comes back. They often become rich because of their original ideas.

Their most fortunate colors are all shades of green, white and yellow. They should avoid all dark colors whenever possible.

Their lucky jewels are the "cat's eyes", pearls and moonstones. They should wear a piece of moonstone next to their flesh.

BIRTH DATE: 8 - 17 - 26

Most number -8- people are go-getters, who believe that you never get a second chance to make a good first impression. They have deep and intense natures, and also great strength of individuality. They don't wait for their ship to come in, they swim out to meet it. They often appear undemonstrative, but in reality they have warm hearts, especially towards the oppressed of all classes. They strive to ensure the success of their children, and teach them the value of money at an early age. They like demanding assignments, are very organized, and will stay on the job as long as they feel there is a future. If ambitious, they generally hold a high position. According to number 8, winning isn't everything, it's the only thing.

Their most fortunate colors are grey and blue, black and

purple. All dark shades of colors.

Their lucky jewels are the amethyst, dark sapphire, black pearl or the black diamond. Whenever possible, they should wear one of these next to their skin.

BIRTH DATE: 9 - 18 - 27

Number -9- people are optimists, who live in the present and let go of the past. "Brotherly love" has real meaning to these humanitarians, so they give without remembering and take without forgetting. They are sociable and like good food and fine music. There's always room for one more in their home. Number 9 individuals see beauty and potential in everyone and everything. They are strong-willed and fighters in all they attempt in life. They are impulsive, independent, and have the power to influence individuals from all walks of life. They are also resourceful and excellent in organization, providing they have the fullest control. They resent criticism, and usually have a good opinion of themselves.

Their most fortunate colors are all shades of crimson or red, and all rose and pink tones.

Their lucky jewels are the ruby, garnet and blood stone. They should wear one of these stones next to their skin.

KEY YEARLY MESSAGE

Numbers assigned to each
Month:

January 1
February 2
March........................3
April............................4
May..............................5
June............................ 6
July.............................. 7
August......................... 8
September....................9
October...10=................1
November...11=............2
December...12=.............3
Year:
1998 = 27 = 9
(1+9+9+8) = 27 (2+7) = 9
1999 = 28 = 1
2000 =......... 2
2001=...........3

To determine your key message for this year or any other year, proceed as follows; add your birth date number, and your birth month number, to the current year number.

Example: Birth date February 19th. (Since February is the second month, it counts for 2)

$$2+19+1998=39=12=3$$

$$2+ (1+9) + (1+9+9+8) = 39 (3+9) = 12 (1+2) = 3$$

In this case, your yearly message would be found in No. 3.

There is a rhythm to life based on nine-year cycles. Knowing which year of the cycle you are in, can give you a sense of where you belong in the scheme of things. It will shed some light on your main message for this year, and years to come. You will know when to anchor, when to set sail, and most important, when your ship is coming in.

YEAR NUMBER 1

This is the beginning of a new nine-year cycle. You make a fresh start and it's time for action. The seeds you plant now will determine your future harvest. Bear this in mind throughout the year. Believe in yourself, cultivate a new attitude, and go after what you want.

YEAR NUMBER 2

Do not take things too personally this year, as you might be a little too sensitive. This could be a waiting time. Togetherness and partnership are accented. Study something of interest or take up a hobby or a sport. Do not dwell on your fears. Do the little things this year and avoid making hasty decisions.

YEAR NUMBER 3

This could be a great year to communicate your ideas in spoken or written form. Create and reap the seeds you have sown. There will be a lot to do and your energy may be scattered. Socialize and enjoy family and friends. It's a period of expansion, so make the most of it. Good fortune is coming your way.

YEAR NUMBER 4

This year represents a lot of hard work. You could feel restricted and bored at times. However, keep your nose to the grindstone, and build a firm foundation for the future. Throw in some fun and relaxation, and adequate rest. Learn from past mistakes and watch your finances.

YEAR NUMBER 5

Expect the unexpected this year. It's time to get out of the rut and enjoy yourself. You'll experience fun, freedom, changes, and you will probably want to travel. Make the most out of life and new opportunities. Be more flexible and spontaneous.

YEAR NUMBER 6

A year centered around love, home and family. Responsibilities and adjustments play a big role. You may decide to beautify yourself or your surroundings. You should have no problem attracting people. Feel the needs of others, be fair, and keep your word.

YEAR NUMBER 7

This is the year to take time for yourself. Read interesting books, get closer to nature, do the things you like to do. Think about where you have been, and where you are heading in life. Analyze and get to know yourself better. Dig deeply for answers, and rely on your intuition.

YEAR NUMBER 8

Pull out all stops! This is the time for money, power and success. Balance yourself mentally and physically to assure good health. You will need to be organized for what's ahead this year. Get your finances in order, and capitalize on lucrative business deals.

YEAR NUMBER 9

This is the last year of this cycle. Time to weed your garden and discard things that are no longer useful. Let go of past disappointments, as a new door will open next year. Sharing and thinking of others will help. Life is a boomerang; what goes around, comes around.

ARIES

There is no getting away from the fact, that there are only nine numbers by which all our calculations on this earth are made. Beyond these nine numbers, all the rest are repetition, as 10 is a 1 with a 0 added, eleven (11) is $1 + 1 = 2$; and so on. Every number, no matter how high, can be reduced to a single figure. This is why your lucky numbers first appear as single numbers, followed by numbers adding up to this single number, up to 31. However, any number over 31 which adds up to any of your single lucky numbers, is also lucky for you.

Your first lucky number is - 4 - and all numbers adding up to 4, such as 13-22-31 - Lucky day Sunday. This number was determined by combining your celestial number with other factors of your sun sign.

Your luckiest number is 4. Bear this in mind at all times. When you buy a ticket of any sort, make sure that the serial number has the predominant number 4 in it, and buy it during one of your lucky periods. Also a street address containing one or more 4's; horse number 4, player number 4 in a game; a 4 rolled in dice; room number 4 in a hotel/motel; and so on. These are all considered fortunate for you. You can also combine number 4 with your other lucky numbers.

Your second lucky number is your birth date.

Your third lucky number is - 9 - as well as 18 and 27 - Lucky day Tuesday. This is the number assigned to the planet Mars, ruler of Aries.

NOTE: Since number 9 is part of the 3-6-9 combination, you will have a certain degree of luck with 3-12-21-30 (lucky day Thursday) and 6-15-24 (lucky day Friday). All these numbers are especially lucky on Tuesday, Thursday and Friday.

BIRTH DATES

NUMBERS: 1 - 10 - 19 - 28
LUCKY DAYS: Sunday and Monday

People born on one of these dates are fortunate, because these numbers are related to 4-13-22-31 (lucky day Sunday), and the series of 1 and 4 are interrelated to 2-11-20-29 and 7-16-25 (lucky day Monday). Therefore, all these numbers are especially lucky on Sunday and Monday.

Your lucky yearly periods are; July 20th to August 28th and March 21st to April 28th.

NUMBERS: 2 - 11 - 20 - 29
LUCKY DAYS: Monday and Sunday

People born on one of these dates are fortunate, because these numbers are related to 7-16-25 (lucky day Monday), and the series of 2 and 7 are interrelated to 1-10-19-28 and 4-13-22-31 (lucky day Sunday). Therefore, all these numbers are especially lucky on Monday and Sunday.

Your lucky yearly period is from June 21st to July 27th.

NUMBERS: 3 - 12 - 21 - 30
LUCKY DAY: Thursday

NOTE: Since these numbers are part of the 3-6-9 combination, you will have a certain degree of luck with 6-15-24 (lucky day Friday) and 9-18-27 (lucky day Tuesday). All these numbers are especially lucky on Thursday, Tuesday and Friday.

Your lucky yearly periods are; February 19th to March 27th and November 21st to December 27th.

NUMBERS: 4 - 13 - 22 - 31
LUCKY DAYS: Sunday and Monday.

If one of these dates is your birth date, these numbers are extremely lucky for you, since they happen to be the same as your first lucky number.

You are fortunate, because these numbers are related to 1-10-19-28 (lucky day Sunday), and the series of 4 and 1 are interrelated to 2-11-20-29 and 7-16-25 (lucky day Monday).Therefore, all these numbers are especially lucky on Sunday and Monday.

Your lucky yearly period is from June 21st to August 30th.

NUMBERS: 5 - 14 - 23
LUCKY DAY: Wednesday

You will also have a certain degree of luck on Fridays.

Your lucky yearly periods are; May 21st to June 27th and August 21st to September 27th.

NUMBERS: 6 - 15 - 24
LUCKY DAY: Friday

NOTE: Since these numbers are part of the 3-6-9 combination, you will have a certain degree of luck with 3-12-21-30 (lucky day Thursday) and 9-18-27 (lucky day Tuesday). All these numbers are especially lucky on Friday, Tuesday and Thursday.

Your lucky yearly periods are; April 20th to May 27th and September 21st to October 27th.

NUMBERS: 7 - 16 - 25
LUCKY DAYS: Monday and Sunday.

People born on one of these dates are fortunate, because these numbers are related to 2-11-20-29 (lucky day Monday), and the series of 7 and 2 are interrelated to 1-10-19-28 and 4-13-22-31 (lucky day Sunday). Therefore, all these numbers are especially lucky on Monday and Sunday.

Your lucky yearly period is from June 21st to July 27th, and less strongly from this date to the end of August.

NUMBERS: 8 - 17 - 26
LUCKY DAY: Saturday

Since number 8 has a connection to number 4, you could have a certain degree of luck on Sundays.

Your lucky yearly periods are; from December 21st to December 31st, all of January up to February 26th.

NUMBERS: 9 - 18 - 27
LUCKY DAY: Tuesday

If one of these dates is your birth date, these numbers are extremely lucky for you since they happen to be the same as your third lucky number.

NOTE: Since these numbers are part of the 3-6-9 combination, you will have a certain degree of luck with 3-12-21-30 (lucky day Thursday) and 6-15-24 (lucky day Friday). All these numbers are especially lucky on Tuesday, Thursday and Friday.

Your lucky yearly periods are; March 21st to April 27th and October 21st to November 27th.

DECANS

Note: Decans are Stars or Constellations that rise once every ten days and by which the ancient Egyptians used to tell time.

There are certain periods during the year that are most fortunate for you, when your chances of winning are amplified even more.

If you were born on March 21, 22, 23, 24, 25, 26, 27, 28, 29, 30 - the following periods are lucky for you:
January 21st to 31st
May 21st to 31st
July 23rd to August 3rd
November 23rd to December 3rd

If you were born on April 1, 2, 3, 4, 5, 6, 7, 8, 9, 10 - the following periods are lucky for you:

February 1st to 11th

June 1st to 12th

August 3rd to 14th

December 2nd to 13th

If you were born on April 11, 12, 13, 14, 15, 16, 17, 18, 19, 20 - the following periods are lucky for you:

February 9th to 20th

June 10th to 21st

August 12th to 23rd

December 11th to 23rd

The lucky periods in your Personal Luck Chart, and your lucky numbers, remain the same for the rest of your life. They are based on your birth date and the time of sunrise, which varies greatly throughout the year. I have provided you with sunrise times from 3:00 a.m. to 9:00 a.m. Your lucky hours have been indicated for each hour of sunrise, for each day of the week. The only thing that changes is the time of sunrise, so all you have to do is check the sunrise time on any given day of the year, and go by the lucky hours listed for that time and day. For this reason, it doesn't matter if it's standard or daylight savings time. It also doesn't matter if you are at home or in another part of the world. Just go by the sunrise time for the location you are in, to determine your lucky hours.

SAMPLE

SUNRISE	SUNDAY	MONDAY	TUESDAY
3:00 AM **to** **3:29 AM**	2:00 AM - 5:00 AM 9:00 AM - 12:00 PM 4:00 PM - 7:00 PM 11:00 PM - 2:00 AM	6:00 AM - 9:00 AM 1:00 PM - 4:00 PM 8:00 PM - 11:00 PM	3:00 AM - 6:00 AM 10:00 AM - 1:00 PM 5:00 PM - 8:00 PM 12:00 AM - 3:00 AM
3:30 AM **to** **3:59 AM**	2:30 AM - 5:30 AM 9:30 AM - 12:30 PM 4:30 PM -7:30 PM 11:30 PM - 2:30 AM	6:30 AM - 9:30 AM 1:30 PM - 4:30 PM 8:30 PM - 11:30 PM	3:30 AM - 6:30 AM 10:30 AM - 1:30 PM 5:30 PM - 8:30 PM 12:30 AM - 3:30 AM
4:00 AM **to** **4:29 AM**	3:00 AM - 6:00 AM 10:00 AM - 1:00 PM 5:00 PM - 8:00 PM 12:00 AM - 3:00 AM	7:00 AM - 10:00 AM 2:00 PM - 5:00 PM 9:00 PM - 12:00 AM	*4:00 AM -7:00 AM* *11:00 AM - 2:00 PM* *6:00 PM - 9:00 PM* *1:00 AM - 4:00 AM*
4:30 AM **to** **4:59 AM**	3:30 AM - 6:30 AM 10:30 AM - 1:30 PM 5:30 PM - 8:30 PM 12:30 AM - 3:30 AM	7:30 AM - 10:30 AM 2:30 PM - 5:30 PM 9:30 PM - 12:30 AM	4:30 AM -7:30 AM 11:30 AM - 2:30 PM 6:30 PM - 9:30 PM 1:30 AM - 4:30 AM
5:00 AM **to** **5:29 AM**	4:00 AM - 7:00 AM 11:00 AM - 2:00 PM 6:00 PM - 9:00 PM 1:00 AM - 4:00 AM	8:00 AM - 11:00 AM 3:00 PM - 6:00 PM 10:00 PM - 1:00 AM	5:00 AM - 8:00 AM 12:00 PM - 3:00 PM 7:00 PM - 10:00 PM 2:00 AM - 5:00 AM
5:30 AM **to** **5:59 AM**	4:30 AM - 7:30 AM 11:30 AM - 2:30 PM 6:30 PM - 9:30 PM 1:30 AM - 4:30 AM	8:30 AM - 11:30 AM 3:30 PM - 6:30 PM 10:30 PM - 1:30 AM	5:30 AM - 8:30 AM 12:30 PM - 3:30 PM 7:30 PM - 10:30 PM 2:30 AM - 5:30 AM

For those of you who are not familiar with charts, here is an example. **Example:** Sunrise is 4:15 a.m. on Tuesday.

      Go to the left column under "Sunrise" and choose the time frame "4:00 a.m.-4:29 a.m." Follow in a straight line to the right until you are under Tuesday. The four lucky time periods on this day are shown as 4:00-7:00 a.m., 11:00 a.m.-2:00 p.m., 6:00-9:00 p.m., and 1:00-4:00 a.m. However, if sunrise is 4:15 a.m., the lucky hours would then become 4:15-7:15 a.m., 11:15

LUCK CHART

WEDNESDAY	THURSDAY	FRIDAY	SATURDAY
7:00 AM - 10:00 AM 2:00 PM - 5:00 PM 9:00 PM - 12:00 AM	4:00 AM - 7:00 AM 11:00 AM - 2:00 PM 6:00 PM - 9:00 PM 1:00 AM - 4:00 AM	8:00 AM - 11:00 AM 3:00 PM - 6:00 PM 10:00 PM - 1:00 AM	5:00 AM - 8:00 AM 12:00 PM - 3:00 PM 7:00 PM - 10:00 PM
7:30 AM - 10:30 AM 2:30 PM - 5:30 PM 9:30 PM - 12:30 AM	4:30 AM - 7:30 AM 11:30 AM - 2:30 PM 6:30 PM - 9:30 PM 1:30 AM - 4:30 AM	8:30 AM - 11:30 AM 3:30 PM - 6:30 PM 10:30 PM - 1:30 AM	5:30 AM - 8:30 AM 12:30 PM - 3:30 PM 7:30 PM - 10:30 PM
8:00 AM - 11:00 AM 3:00 PM - 6:00 PM 10:00 PM - 1:00 AM	5:00 AM - 8:00 AM 12:00 PM - 3:00 PM 7:00 PM - 10:00 PM 2:00 AM - 5:00 AM	9:00 AM - 12:00 PM 4:00 PM - 7:00 PM 11:00 PM - 2:00 AM	6:00 AM - 9:00 AM 1:00 PM - 4:00 PM 8:00 PM - 11:00 PM
8:30 AM - 11:30 AM 3:30 PM - 6:30 PM 10:30 PM - 1:30 AM	5:30 AM - 8:30 AM 12:30 PM - 3:30 PM 7:30 PM - 10:30 PM 2:30 AM - 5:30 AM	9:30 AM - 12:30 PM 4:30 PM - 7:30 PM 11:30 PM - 2:30 PM	6:30 AM -9:30 AM 1:30 PM - 4:30 PM 8:30 PM - 11:30 PM
9:00 AM - 12:00 PM 4:00 PM - 7:00 PM 11:00 PM - 2:00 AM	6:00 AM - 9:00 AM 1:00 PM - 4:00 PM 8:00 PM - 11:00 PM 3:00 AM - 6:00 AM	10:00 AM - 1:00 PM 5:00 PM - 8:00 PM 12:00 PM - 3:00 AM	7:00 AM - 10:00 AM 2:00 PM - 5:00 PM 9:00 PM - 12:00 AM
9:30 AM - 12:30 PM 4:30 PM - 7:30 PM 11:30 PM - 2:30 AM	6:30 AM -9:30 AM 1:30 PM - 4:30 PM 8:30 PM - 11:30 PM 3:30 AM - 6:30 AM	10:30 AM - 1:30 PM 5:30 PM - 8:30 PM 12:30 AM - 3:30 AM	7:30 AM - 10:30 AM 2:30 PM - 5:30 PM 9:30 PM - 12:30 AM

a.m.-2:15 p.m., 6:15 to 9:15 p.m. and 1:15 to 4:15 a.m. The middle hour is the most powerful, so in the case of the first lucky period, it would be 5:15-6:15 a.m., and so on.

As I suggested at the beginning, it is important to transfer all your personal luck information onto a calendar, so that you will be able to tell at a glance, what your lucky days, lucky periods and lucky numbers are every month. It involves very little time and it's worth it.

Refer to the *Chapter 2* - "Preparing a luck calendar".

ARIES PERSONAL

SUNRISE	SUNDAY	MONDAY	TUESDAY
3:00 AM to 3:29 AM	8:00 AM - 11:00 AM 3:00 PM - 6:00 PM 10:00 PM - 1:00 AM	5:00 AM - 8:00 AM 12:00 PM - 3:00 PM 7:00 PM - 10:00 PM	2:00 AM - 5:00 AM 9:00 AM - 12:00 PM 4:00 PM - 7:00 PM 11:00 PM - 2:00 AM
3:30 AM to 3:59 AM	8:30 AM - 11:30 AM 3:30 PM - 6:30 PM 10:30 PM - 1:30 AM	5:30 AM - 8:30 AM 12:30 PM - 3:30 PM 7:30 PM - 10:30 PM	2:30 AM - 5:30 AM 9:30 AM - 12:30 PM 4:30 PM - 7:30 PM 11:30 PM - 2:30 AM
4:00 AM to 4:29 AM	9:00 AM - 12:00 PM 4:00 PM - 7:00 PM 11:00 PM - 2:00 AM	6:00 AM - 9:00 AM 1:00 PM - 4:00 PM 8:00 PM - 11:00 PM	3:00 AM - 6:00 AM 10:00 AM - 1:00 PM 5:00 PM - 8:00 PM 12:00 AM - 3:00 AM
4:30 AM to 4:59 AM	9:30 AM - 12:30 PM 4:30 PM - 7:30 PM 11:30 PM - 2:30 AM	6:30 AM - 9:30 AM 1:30 PM - 4:30 PM 8:30 PM - 11:30 PM	3:30 AM - 6:30 AM 10:30 AM - 1:30 PM 5:30 PM - 8:30 PM 12:30 AM - 3:30 AM
5:00 AM to 5:29 AM	10:00 AM - 1:00 PM 5:00 PM - 8:00 PM 12:00 AM - 3:00 AM	7:00 AM - 10:00 AM 2:00 PM - 5:00 PM 9:00 PM - 12:00 AM	4:00 AM -7:00 AM 11:00 AM - 2:00 PM 6:00 PM - 9:00 PM 1:00 AM - 4:00 AM
5:30 AM to 5:59 AM	10:30 AM - 1:30 PM 5:30 PM - 8:30 PM 12:30 AM - 3:30 AM	7:30 AM - 10:30 AM 2:30 PM - 5:30 PM 9:30 PM - 12:30 AM	4:30 AM -7:30 AM 11:30 AM - 2:30 PM 6:30 PM - 9:30 PM 1:30 AM - 4:30 AM

Refer to *Sample Chart* on page *36* for instructions.

LUCK CHART

WEDNESDAY	THURSDAY	FRIDAY	SATURDAY
6:00 AM - 9:00 AM 1:00 PM - 4:00 PM 8:00 PM - 11:00 PM	3:00 AM - 6:00 AM 10:00 AM - 1:00 PM 5:00 PM - 8:00 PM 12:00 AM - 3:00 AM	7:00 AM - 10:00 AM 2:00 PM - 5:00 PM 9:00 PM - 12:00 AM	4:00 AM - 7:00 AM 11:00 AM - 2:00 PM 6:00 PM - 9:00 PM 1:00 AM - 4:00 AM
6:30 AM - 9:30 AM 1:30 PM - 4:30 PM 8:30 PM - 11:30 PM	3:30 AM - 6:30 AM 10:30 AM - 1:30 PM 5:30 PM - 8:30 PM 12:30 AM - 3:30 AM	7:30 AM - 10:30 AM 2:30 PM - 5:30 PM 9:30 PM - 12:30 AM	4:30 AM - 7:30 AM 11:30 AM - 2:30 PM 6:30 PM - 9:30 PM 1:30 AM - 4:30 AM
7:00 AM - 10:00 AM 2:00 PM - 5:00 PM 9:00 PM - 12:00 AM	4:00 AM - 7:00 AM 11:00 AM - 2:00 PM 6:00 PM - 9:00 PM 1:00 AM - 4:00 AM	8:00 AM - 11:00 AM 3:00 PM - 6:00 PM 10:00 PM - 1:00 AM	5:00 AM - 8:00 AM 12:00 PM - 3:00 PM 7:00 PM - 10:00 PM 2:00 AM - 5:00 AM
7:30 AM - 10:30 AM 2:30 PM - 5:30 PM 9:30 PM - 12:30 AM	4:30 AM - 7:30 AM 11:30 AM - 2:30 PM 6:30 PM - 9:30 PM 1:30 AM - 4:30 AM	8:30 AM - 11:30 AM 3:30 PM - 6:30 PM 10:30 PM - 1:30 AM	5:30 AM - 8:30 AM 12:30 PM - 3:30 PM 7:30 PM - 10:30 PM 2:30 AM - 5:30 AM
8:00 AM - 11:00 AM 3:00 PM - 6:00 PM 10:00 PM - 1:00 AM	5:00 AM - 8:00 AM 12:00 PM - 3:00 PM 7:00 PM - 10:00 PM 2:00 AM - 5:00 AM	9:00 AM - 12:00 PM 4:00 PM - 7:00 PM 11:00 PM - 2:00 AM	6:00 AM - 9:00 AM 1:00 PM - 4:00 PM 8:00 PM - 11:00 PM 3:00 AM - 6:00 AM
8:30 AM - 11:30 AM 3:30 PM - 6:30 PM 10:30 PM - 1:30 AM	5:30 AM - 8:30 AM 12:30 PM - 3:30 PM 7:30 PM - 10:30 PM 2:30 AM - 5:30 AM	9:30 AM - 12:30 PM 4:30 PM - 7:30 PM 11:30 PM - 2:30 PM	6:30 AM -9:30 AM 1:30 PM - 4:30 PM 8:30 PM - 11:30 PM 3:30 AM - 6:30 AM

SUNRISE	SUNDAY	MONDAY	TUESDAY
6:00 AM **to** **6:29 AM**	11:00 AM - 2:00 PM 6:00 PM - 9:00 PM 1:00 AM - 4:00 AM	8:00 AM - 11:00 AM 3:00 PM - 6:00 PM 10:00 PM - 1:00 AM	5:00 AM - 8:00 AM 12:00 PM - 3:00 PM 7:00 PM - 10:00 PM 2:00 AM - 5:00 AM
6:30 AM **to** **6:59 AM**	11:30 AM - 2:30 PM 6:30 PM - 9:30 PM 1:30 AM - 4:30 AM	8:30 AM - 11:30 AM 3:30 PM - 6:30 PM 10:30 PM - 1:30 AM	5:30 AM - 8:30 AM 12:30 PM - 3:30 PM 7:30 PM - 10:30 PM 2:30 AM - 5:30 AM
7:00 AM **to** **7:29 AM**	12:00 PM -3:30 PM 7:00 PM - 10:00 PM 2:00 AM - 5:00 AM	9:00 AM - 12:00 PM 4:00 PM - 7:00 PM 11:00 PM - 2:00 AM	6:00 AM - 9:00 AM 1:00 PM - 4:00 PM 8:00 PM - 11:00 PM 3:00 AM - 6:00 AM
7:30 AM **to** **7:59 AM**	12:30 AM -3:30 PM 7:30 PM - 10:30 PM 2:30 AM - 5:30 AM	9:30 AM - 12:30 PM 4:30 PM - 7:30 PM 11:30 PM - 2:30 AM	6:30 AM - 9:30 AM 1:30 PM - 4:30 PM 8:30 PM - 11:30 PM 3:30 AM - 6:30 AM
8:00 AM **to** **8:29 AM**	1:00 PM - 4:00 PM 8:00 PM - 11:00 PM 3:00 AM - 6:00 AM	10:00 AM -1:00 PM 5:00 PM - 8:00 PM 12:00 AM - 3:00 AM	7:00 AM - 10:00 AM 2:00 PM - 5:00 PM 9:00 PM - 12:00 AM
8:30 AM **to** **8:59 AM**	1:30 PM - 4:30 PM 8:30 PM - 11:30 PM 3:30 AM - 6:30 AM	10:30 AM -1:30 PM 5:30 PM - 8:30 PM 12:30 AM - 3:30 AM	7:30 AM - 10:30 AM 2:30 PM - 5:30 PM 9:30 PM - 12:30 AM

WEDNESDAY	THURSDAY	FRIDAY	SATURDAY
9:00 AM - 12:00 PM 4:00 PM -7:00 PM 11:00 PM - 2:00 AM	6:00 AM -9:00 AM 1:00 PM - 4:00 PM 8:00 PM -11:00 PM 3:00 AM - 6:00 AM	10:00 AM - 1:00 PM 5:00 PM - 8:00 PM 12:00 AM -3:00 AM	7:00 AM - 10:00 AM 2:00 PM - 5:00 PM 9:00 PM - 12:00 AM 4:00 AM - 7:00 AM
9:30 AM - 12:30 PM 4:30 PM - 7:30 PM 11:30 PM - 2:30 AM	6:30 AM - 9:30 AM 1:30 PM - 4:30 PM 8:30 PM - 11:30 PM 3:30 AM - 6:30 AM	10:30 AM - 1:30 PM 5:30 PM - 8:30 PM 12:30 AM - 3:30 AM	7:30 AM - 10:30 AM 2:30 PM - 5:30 PM 9:30 PM - 12:30 AM 4:30 AM - 7:30 AM
10:00 AM - 1:00 PM 5:00 PM - 8:00 PM 12:00 AM - 3:00 AM	7:00 AM - 10:00 AM 2:00 PM - 5:00 PM 9:00 PM - 12:00 AM	4:00 AM - 7:00 AM 11:00 AM - 2:00 PM 6:00 PM - 9:00 PM 1:00 AM - 4:00 AM	8:00 AM - 11:00 AM 3:00 PM - 6:00 PM 10:00 PM - 1:00 AM 5:00 AM - 8:00 AM
10:30 AM - 1:30 PM 5:30 PM - 8:30 PM 12:30 AM - 3:30 AM	7:30 AM - 10:30 AM 2:30 PM - 5:30 PM 9:30 PM - 12:30 AM	4:30 AM - 7:30 AM 11:30 AM - 2:30 PM 6:30 PM - 9:30 PM 1:30 AM - 4:30 AM	8:30 AM - 11:30 AM 3:30 PM - 6:30 PM 10:30 PM - 1:30 AM 5:30 AM - 8:30 AM
4:00 AM - 7:00 AM 11:00 AM - 2:00 PM 6:00 PM - 9:00 PM 1:00 AM - 4:00 AM	8:00 AM - 11:00 AM 3:00 PM - 6:00 PM 10:00 PM - 1:00 AM	5:00 AM - 8:00 AM 12:00 AM - 3:00 AM 7:00 PM - 10:00 PM 2:00 AM - 5:00 AM	9:00 AM - 12:00 PM 4:00 PM - 7:00 PM 11:00 PM - 2:00 AM 6:00 AM - 9:00 AM
4:30 AM - 7:30 AM 11:30 AM - 2:30 PM 6:30 PM - 9:30 PM 1:30 AM - 4:30 AM	8:30 AM - 11:30 AM 3:30 PM - 6:30 PM 10:30 PM - 1:30 AM	5:30 AM - 8:30 AM 12:30 PM - 3:30 PM 7:30 PM - 10:30 PM 2:30 AM - 5:30 AM	9:30 AM - 12:30 PM 4:30 PM - 7:30 PM 11:30 PM - 2:30 AM 6:30 AM - 9:30 AM

There is no getting away from the fact, that there are only nine numbers by which all our calculations on this earth are made. Beyond these nine numbers, all the rest are repetition, as 10 is a 1 with a 0 added, eleven (11) is 1+1 = 2; and so on. Every number, no matter how high, can be reduced to a single figure. This is why your lucky numbers first appear as single numbers, followed by numbers adding up to this single number, up to 31. However, any number over 31 which adds up to any of your single lucky numbers, is also lucky for you.

Your first lucky number is - 9 - and all numbers adding up to 9, such as 18 and 27 - Lucky day Tuesday. This number was determined by combining your celestial number with other factors of your sun sign.

Your luckiest number is 9. Bear this in mind at all times. When you buy a ticket of any sort, make sure that the serial number has the predominant number 9 in it, and buy it during one of your lucky periods. Also a street address containing one or more 9's; horse number 9, player number 9 in a game; a 9 rolled in dice; room number 9 in a hotel/motel; and so on. These are all considered fortunate for you. You can also combine number 9 with your other lucky numbers.

Your second lucky number is your birth date.

Your third lucky number is - 6 - as well as 15 and 24 - Lucky day Friday. This is the number assigned to the planet Venus, ruler of Taurus.

NOTE: Since numbers 9 and 6 are part of the 3-6-9 combination, you will have a certain degree of luck with 3-12-21-30 (lucky day Thursday). All these numbers are especially lucky on Tuesday, Thursday and Friday.

BIRTH DATES

NUMBERS: 1 - 10 - 19 - 28
LUCKY DAYS: Sunday and Monday.

People born on one of these dates are fortunate, because these numbers are related to 4-13-22-31 (lucky day Sunday), and the series of 1 and 4 are interrelated to 2-11-20-29 and 7-16-25 (lucky day Monday). Therefore, all these numbers are especially lucky on Sunday and Monday.

Your lucky yearly periods are; July 20th to August 28th and March 21st to April 28th.

NUMBERS: 2 - 11 - 20 - 29
LUCKY DAYS: Monday and Sunday.

People born on one of these dates are fortunate, because these numbers are related to 7-16-25 (lucky day Monday), and the series of 2 and 7 are interrelated to 1-10-19-28 and 4-13-22-31 (lucky day Sunday). Therefore, all these numbers are especially lucky on Monday and Sunday.

Your lucky yearly period is from June 21st to July 27th.

NUMBERS: 3 - 12 - 21 - 30
LUCKY DAY: Thursday

NOTE: Since these numbers are part of the 3-6-9 combination, you will have a certain degree of luck with 6-15-24 (lucky day Friday) and 9-18-27 (lucky day Tuesday). All these

numbers are especially lucky on Thursday, Tuesday and Friday.

Your lucky yearly periods are; February 19th to March 27th and November 21st to December 27th.

NUMBERS: 4 - 13 - 22 - 31
LUCKY DAY: Sunday and Monday.

People born on one of these dates are fortunate, because these numbers are related to 1-10-19-28 (lucky day Sunday), and the series of 4 and 1 are interrelated to 2-11-20-29 and 7-16-25 (lucky day Monday). Therefore, all these numbers are especially lucky on Sunday and Monday.

Your lucky yearly period is from June 21st to August 30th.

NUMBERS: 5 - 14 - 23
LUCKY DAY: Wednesday

You will also have a certain degree of luck on Fridays.

Your lucky yearly periods are; May 21st to June 27th and August 21st to September 27th.

NUMBERS: 6 - 15 - 24
LUCKY DAY: Friday

If one of these dates is your birth date, these numbers are extremely lucky for you, since they happen to be the same as your third lucky numbers.

NOTE: Since these numbers are part of the 3-6-9 combination, you will have a certain degree of luck with 3-12-21-30 (lucky day Thursday) and 9-18-27 (lucky day Tuesday). All these numbers are especially lucky on Friday, Tuesday and Thursday.

Your lucky yearly periods are; April 20th to May 27th and September 21st to October 27th.

NUMBERS: 7 - 16 - 25
LUCKY DAYS: Monday and Sunday.

People born on one of these dates are fortunate, because these numbers are related to 2-11-20-29 (lucky day Monday) and the series of 7 and 2 are interrelated to 1-10-19-28 and

4-13-22-31 (lucky day Sunday). Therefore, all these numbers are especially lucky on Monday and Sunday.

Your lucky yearly period is from June 21st to July 27th and less strongly from this date to the end of August.

NUMBERS: 8 - 17 - 26
LUCKY DAY: Saturday

Since number 8 has a connection to number 4, you could have a certain degree of luck on Sundays.

Your lucky yearly periods are; from December 21st to December 31st, all of January up to February 26th.

NUMBERS: 9 - 18 - 27
LUCKY DAY: Tuesday

If one of these dates is your birth date, these numbers are extremely lucky for you since they happen to be the same as your first lucky number.

NOTE: Since these numbers are part of the 3-6-9 combination, you will have a certain degree of luck with 3-12-21-30 (lucky day Thursday) and 6-15-24 (lucky day Friday). All these numbers are especially lucky on Tuesday Thursday and Friday.

Your lucky yearly periods are; March 21st to April 27th and October 21st to November 27th.

DECANS

Note: Decans are Stars or Constellations that rise once every ten days and by which the ancient Egyptians used to tell time.

There are certain periods during the year that are most fortunate for you, when your chances of winning are amplified even more.

If you were born on April 21, 22, 23, 24, 25, 26, 27, 28, 29, 30 and May 1 - the following periods are lucky for you:

February 20th to March 1st
June 22nd to July 3rd

August 24th to September 4th
December 23rd to January 3rd

If you were born on May 2, 3, 4, 5, 6, 7, 8, 9, 10, 11 - the following periods are lucky for you:
January 2nd to January 12th
March 1st to 11th
July 2nd to 13th
September 2nd to 14th

If you were born on May 12, 13, 14, 15, 16, 17, 18, 19, 20, 21 - the following periods are lucky for you.
January 10th to 20th
March 11th to 20th
July 12th to 23rd
September 12th to 23rd

The lucky periods in your Personal Luck Chart, and your lucky numbers, remain the same for the rest of your life. They are based on your birth date and the time of sunrise, which varies greatly throughout the year. I have provided you with sunrise times from 3:00 a.m. to 9:00 a.m. Your lucky hours have been indicated for each hour of sunrise, for each day of the week. The only thing that changes is the time of sunrise, so all you have to do is check the sunrise time on any given day of the year, and go by the lucky hours listed for that time and day. For this reason, it doesn't matter if it's standard or daylight savings time. It also doesn't matter if you are at home or in another part of the world. Just go by the sunrise time for the location you are in, to determine your lucky hours.

Refer to *Sample Chart* on page *36* for instructions.

TAURUS PERSONAL

SUNRISE	SUNDAY	MONDAY	TUESDAY
3:00 AM **to** **3:29 AM**	3:00 AM - 6:00 AM 10:00 AM - 1:00 PM 5:00 PM - 8:00 PM 12:00 AM - 3:00 AM	7:00 AM - 10:00 AM 2:00 PM - 5:00 PM 9:00 PM - 12:00 AM	4:00 AM -7:00 AM 11:00 AM - 2:00 PM 6:00 PM - 9:00 PM
3:30 AM **to** **3:59 AM**	3:30 AM - 6:30 AM 10:30 AM - 1:30 PM 5:30 PM - 8:30 PM 12:30 AM - 3:30 AM	7:30 AM - 10:30 AM 2:30 PM - 5:30 PM 9:30 PM - 12:30 AM	4:30 AM -7:30 AM 11:30 AM - 2:30 PM 6:30 PM - 9:30 PM
4:00 AM **to** **4:29 AM**	4:00 AM -7:00 AM 11:00 AM - 2:00 PM 6:00 PM - 9:00 PM 1:00 AM - 4:00 AM	8:00 AM - 11:00 AM 3:00 PM - 6:00 PM 10:00 PM - 1:00 AM	5:00 AM - 8:00 AM 12:00 PM - 3:00 PM 7:00 PM - 10:00 PM
4:30 AM **to** **4:59 AM**	4:30 AM -7:30 AM 11:30 AM - 2:30 PM 6:30 PM - 9:30 PM 1:30 AM - 4:30 AM	8:30 AM - 11:30 AM 3:30 PM - 6:30 PM 10:30 PM - 1:30 AM	5:30 AM - 8:30 AM 12:30 PM - 3:30 PM 7:30 PM - 10:30 PM
5:00 AM **to** **5:29 AM**	5:00 AM - 8:00 AM 12:00 PM - 3:00 PM 7:00 PM - 10:00 PM 2:00 AM - 5:00 AM	9:00 AM - 12:00 PM 4:00 PM - 7:00 PM 11:00 PM - 2:00 AM	6:00 AM - 9:00 AM 1:00 PM - 4:00 PM 8:00 PM - 11:00 PM
5:30 AM **to** **5:59 AM**	5:30 AM - 8:30 AM 12:30 PM - 3:30 PM 7:30 PM - 10:30 PM 2:30 AM - 5:30 AM	9:30 AM - 12:30 PM 4:30 PM -7:30 PM 11:30 PM - 2:30 AM	6:30 AM - 9:30 AM 1:30 PM - 4:30 PM 8:30 PM - 11:30 PM

Refer to **Sample Chart** on page **36** for instructions.

LUCK CHART

WEDNESDAY	THURSDAY	FRIDAY	SATURDAY
8:00 AM - 11:00 AM 3:00 PM - 6:00 PM 10:00 PM - 1:00 AM	5:00 AM - 8:00 AM 12:00 PM - 3:00 PM 7:00 PM - 10:00 PM	2:00 AM - 5:00 AM 9:00 AM - 12:00 AM 4:00 PM - 7:00 PM 11:00 PM - 2:00 AM	6:00 AM - 9:00 AM 1:00 PM - 4:00 PM 8:00 PM - 11:00 PM
8:30 AM - 11:30 AM 3:30 PM - 6:30 PM 10:30 PM - 1:30 AM	5:30 AM - 8:30 AM 12:30 PM - 3:30 PM 7:30 PM - 10:30 PM	2:30 AM - 5:30 AM 9:30 AM - 12:30 PM 4:30 PM - 7:30 PM 11:30 PM - 2:30 AM	6:30 AM -9:30 AM 1:30 PM - 4:30 PM 8:30 PM - 11:30 PM
9:00 AM - 12:00 PM 4:00 PM - 7:00 PM 11:00 PM - 2:00 AM	6:00 AM - 9:00 AM 1:00 PM - 4:00 PM 8:00 PM - 11:00 PM	3:00 AM - 6:00 AM 10:00 AM - 1:00 PM 5:00 PM - 8:00 PM 12:00 PM - 3:00 AM	7:00 AM - 10:00 AM 2:00 PM - 5:00 PM 9:00 PM - 12:00 AM
9:30 AM - 12:30 PM 4:30 PM - 7:30 PM 11:30 PM - 2:30 AM	6:30 AM -9:30 AM 1:30 PM - 4:30 PM 8:30 PM - 11:30 PM	3:30 AM - 6:30 AM 10:30 AM - 1:30 PM 5:30 PM - 8:30 PM 12:30 AM - 3:30 AM	7:30 AM - 10:30 AM 2:30 PM - 5:30 PM 9:30 PM - 12:30 AM
10:00 AM - 1:00 PM 5:00 PM - 8:00 PM 12:00 PM - 3:00 AM	7:00 AM - 10:00 AM 2:00 PM - 5:00 PM 9:00 PM - 12:00 AM	4:00 AM - 7:00 AM 11:00 AM - 2:00 PM 6:00 PM - 9:00 PM 1:00 AM - 4:00 AM	8:00 AM - 11:00 AM 3:00 PM - 6:00 PM 10:00 PM - 1:00 AM
10:30 AM - 1:30 PM 5:30 PM - 8:30 PM 12:30 AM - 3:30 AM	7:30 AM - 10:30 AM 2:30 PM - 5:30 PM 9:30 PM - 12:30 AM	4:30 AM - 7:30 AM 11:30 AM - 2:30 PM 6:30 PM -9:30 PM 1:30 AM - 4:30 AM	8:30 AM - 11:30 AM 3:30 PM - 6:30 PM 10:30 PM - 1:30 AM

SUNRISE	SUNDAY	MONDAY	TUESDAY
6:00 AM to **6:29 AM**	6:00 AM - 9:00 AM 1:00 PM - 4:00 PM 8:00 PM - 11:00 PM 3:00 AM - 6:00 AM	10:00 AM - 1:00 PM 5:00 PM - 8:00 PM 12:00 AM - 3:00 AM	7:00 AM - 10:00 AM 2:00 PM - 5:00 PM 9:00 PM - 12:00 AM
6:30 AM to **6:59 AM**	6:30 AM - 9:30 AM 1:30 PM - 4:30 PM 8:30 PM - 11:30 PM 3:30 AM - 6:30 AM	10:30 AM - 1:30 PM 5:30 PM - 8:30 PM 12:30 AM - 3:30 AM	7:30 AM - 10:30 AM 2:30 PM - 5:30 PM 9:30 PM - 12:30 AM
7:00 AM to **7:29 AM**	7:00 AM - 10:00 AM 2:00 PM - 5:00 PM 9:00 PM - 12:00 AM	4:00 AM - 7:00 AM 11:00 AM - 2:00 PM 6:00 PM - 9:00 PM 1:00 AM - 4:00 AM	8:00 AM - 11:00 AM 3:00 PM - 6:00 PM 10:00 PM - 1:00 AM
7:30 AM to **7:59 AM**	7:30 AM - 10:30 AM 2:30 PM - 5:30 PM 9:30 PM - 12:30 AM	4:30 AM - 7:30 AM 11:30 AM - 2:30 PM 6:30 PM - 9:30 PM 1:30 AM - 4:30 AM	8:30 AM - 11:30 AM 3:30 PM - 6:30 PM 10:30 PM - 1:30 AM
8:00 AM to **8:29 AM**	8:00 AM - 11:00 AM 3:00 PM - 6:00 PM 10:00 PM - 1:00 AM	5:00 AM - 8:00 AM 12:00 PM - 3:00 PM 7:00 PM - 10:00 PM 2:00 AM - 5:00 AM	9:00 AM - 12:00 PM 4:00 PM - 7:00 PM 11:00 PM - 2:00 AM
8:30 AM to **8:59 AM**	8:30 AM - 11:30 AM 3:30 PM - 6:30 PM 10:30 PM - 1:30 AM	5:30 AM - 8:30 AM 12:30 PM - 3:30 PM 7:30 PM - 10:30 PM 2:30 AM - 5:30 AM	9:30 AM - 12:30 PM 4:30 PM - 7:30 PM 11:30 PM - 2:30 AM

WEDNESDAY	THURSDAY	FRIDAY	SATURDAY
11:00 AM - 2:00 PM 6:00 PM - 9:00 PM 1:00 AM - 4:00 AM	8:00 AM - 11:00 AM 3:00 PM - 6:00 PM 10:00 PM - 1:00 AM	5:00 AM - 8:00 AM 12:00 PM - 3:00 PM 7:00 PM - 10:00 AM 2:00 AM - 5:00 AM	9:00 AM - 12:00 PM 4:00 PM - 7:00 PM 11:00 PM - 2:00 AM
11:30 AM - 2:30 PM 6:30 PM - 9:30 PM 1:30 AM - 4:30 AM	8:30 AM - 11:30 AM 3:30 PM - 6:30 PM 10:30 PM - 1:30 AM	5:30 AM - 8:30 AM 12:30 PM - 3:30 PM 7:30 PM - 10:30 AM 2:30 AM - 5:30 AM	9:30 AM - 12:30 PM 4:30 PM - 7:30 PM 11:30 PM - 2:30 AM
12:00 PM - 3:00 PM 7:00 PM - 10:00 PM 2:00 AM - 5:00 AM	9:00 AM - 12:00 PM 4:00 PM - 7:00 PM 11:00 PM - 2:00 AM	6:00 AM - 9:00 AM 1:00 PM - 4:00 PM 8:00 PM -11:00 AM 3:00 AM - 6:00 AM	10:00 AM - 1:00 PM 5:00 PM - 8:00 PM 12:00 AM - 3:00 AM
12:30 PM - 3:30 PM 7:30 PM - 10:30 PM 2:30 AM - 5:30 AM	9:30 AM - 12:30 PM 4:30 PM - 7:30 PM 11:30 PM - 2:30 AM	6:30 AM - 9:30 AM 1:30 PM - 4:30 PM 8:30 PM - 11:30 AM 3:30 AM - 6:30 AM	10:30 AM - 1:30 PM 5:30 PM - 8:30 PM 12:30 AM - 3:30 AM
1:00 PM - 4:00 PM 8:00 PM -11:00 AM 3:00 AM - 6:00 AM	10:00 AM - 1:00 PM 5:00 PM - 8:00 PM 12:00 AM - 3:00 AM	7:00 AM - 10:00 AM 2:00 PM - 5:00 PM 9:00 PM - 12:00 PM 4:00 AM - 7:00 AM	11:00 AM - 2:00 PM 6:00 PM - 9:00 PM 1:00 AM - 4:00 AM
1:30 PM - 4:30 PM 8:30 PM - 11:30 PM 3:30 AM - 6:30 AM	10:30 AM - 1:30 PM 5:30 PM - 8:30 PM 12:30 AM - 3:30 AM	7:30 AM - 10:30 AM 2:30 PM - 5:30 PM 9:30 PM - 12:30 PM 4:30 AM - 7:30 AM	11:30 AM - 2:30 PM 6:30 PM - 9:30 PM 1:30 AM - 4:30 AM

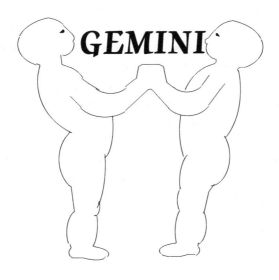

GEMINI

There is no getting away from the fact, that there are only nine numbers by which all our calculations on this earth are made. Beyond these nine numbers, all the rest are repetition, as 10 is a 1 with a 0 added, eleven (11) is 1+1= 2; and so on. Every number, no matter how high, can be reduced to a single figure. That is why your lucky numbers first appear as single numbers, followed by numbers adding up to this single number, up to 31. However, any number over 31 which adds up to any of your single lucky numbers, is also lucky for you.

Your first lucky number is - 7 - and all numbers adding up to 7, such as 16 and 25 - Lucky day Monday. This number was determined by combining your celestial number with other factors of your sun sign.

Your luckiest number is 7. Bear this in mind at all times. When you buy a ticket of any sort, make sure that the serial number has the predominant number 7 in it, and buy it during one of your lucky periods. Also a street address containing one or more 7's; horse number 7, player number 7 in a game; a 7 rolled in dice; room number 7 in a hotel/motel; and so on. These are all considered fortunate for you. You can also combine number 7 with your other lucky numbers.

Your second lucky number is your birth date.

Your third lucky number is - 5 - as well as 14 and 23 - Lucky day Wednesday. This is the number assigned to the planet Mercury, ruler of Gemini.

BIRTH DATES

NUMBERS: 1 - 10 - 19 - 28
LUCKY DAYS: Sunday and Monday

People born on one of these dates are fortunate, because these numbers are related to 4-13-22-31 (lucky day Sunday), and the series of 1 and 4 are interrelated to 2-11-20-29 and 7-16-25 (lucky day Monday). Therefore, all these numbers are especially lucky on Sunday and Monday.

Your lucky yearly periods are; July 20th to August 28th and March 21st to April 28th.

NUMBERS: 2 - 11 - 20 - 29
LUCKY DAYS: Monday and Sunday.

People born on one of these dates are fortunate, because these numbers are related to 7-16- 25 (lucky day Monday), and the series of 2 and 7 are interrelated to 1-10-19-28 and 4-13-22-31 (lucky day Sunday). Therefore, all these numbers are especially lucky on Monday and Sunday.

Your lucky yearly period is from June 21st to July 27th.

NUMBERS: 3 - 12 - 21 - 30
LUCKY DAY: Thursday
NOTE: Since these numbers are part of the 3-6-9 combination, you will have a certain degree of luck with 6-15-24 (lucky day Friday) and 9-18-27 (lucky day Tuesday). All these numbers are especially lucky on Thursday, Tuesday and Friday.

Your lucky yearly periods are; February 19th to March 27th and November 21st to December 27th.

NUMBERS: 4 - 13 - 22 - 31
LUCKY DAYS: Sunday and Monday.
People born on one of these dates are fortunate, because these numbers are related to 1-10-19-28 (lucky day Sunday), and the series of 4 and 1 are interrelated to 2-11-20-29 and 7-16-25 (lucky day Monday). Therefore, all these numbers are especially lucky on Sunday and Monday.

Your lucky yearly period is from June 21st to August 30th.

NUMBERS: 5 - 14 - 23
LUCKY DAY: Wednesday
If one of these dates is your birth date, these numbers are extremely lucky for you, since they happen to be the same as your third lucky number. You will also have a certain degree of luck on Fridays.

Your lucky yearly periods are; May 21st to June 27th and August 21st to September 27th.

NUMBERS: 6 - 15 - 24
LUCKY DAY: Friday
NOTE: Since these numbers are part of the 3-6-9 combination, you will have a certain degree of luck with 3-12-21-30 (lucky day Thursday) and 9-18-27 (lucky day Tuesday). All these numbers are especially lucky on Friday, Tuesday and Thursday.

Your lucky yearly periods are; April 20th to May 27th and September 21st to October 27th.

NUMBERS: 7 - 16 - 25
LUCKY DAYS: Monday and Sunday

If one of these dates is your birth date, these numbers are extremely lucky for you, since they happen to be the same as your first lucky number.

People born on one of these dates are fortunate, because these numbers are related to 2-11-20-29 (lucky day Monday), and the series of 7 and 2 are interrelated to 1-10-19-28 and 4-13-22-31 (lucky day Sunday). Therefore, all these numbers are especially lucky on Monday and Sunday.

Your lucky yearly period is from June 21st to July 27th and less strongly from this date to the end of August.

NUMBERS: 8 - 17 - 26
LUCKY DAY: Saturday

Since number 8 has a connection to number 4, you could have a certain degree of luck on Sundays.

Your lucky yearly periods are; from December 21st to December 31st, all of January up to February 26th.

NUMBERS: 9 - 18 - 27
LUCKY DAY: Tuesday

NOTE: Since these numbers are part of the 3-6-9 combination, you will have a certain degree of luck with 3-12-21-30 (lucky day Thursday) and 6-15-24 (lucky day Friday). All these numbers are especially lucky on Tuesday, Thursday and Friday.

Your lucky yearly periods are; March 21st to April 27th and October 21st to November 27th.

DECANS

Note: Decans are Stars or Constellations that rise once every ten days and by which the ancient Egyptians used to tell time.

There are certain periods during the year that are most fortunate for you, when your chances of winning are amplified even more.

If you were born on May 22, 23, 24, 25, 26, 27, 28, 29, 30, 31 and June 1 - the following periods are lucky for you.

January 21st to 30th
March 21st to 31st
July 24th to August 3rd
September 23rd to October 3rd

If you were born on June 2, 3, 4, 5, 6, 7, 8, 9, 10, 11 - the following periods are lucky for you.

January 31st to February 9th
April 1st to 10th
August 4th to 13th
October 4th to 13th

If you were born on June 12, 13, 14, 15, 16, 17, 18, 19, 20, 21 - the following periods are lucky for you.

February 10th to 19th
April 11th to 20th
August 13th to 23rd
October 14th to 23rd

The lucky periods in your Personal Luck Chart, and your lucky numbers, remain the same for the rest of your life. They are based on your birth date and the time of sunrise, which varies greatly throughout the year. I have provided you with sunrise times from 3:00 a.m. to 9:00 a.m. Your lucky hours have been indicated for each hour of sunrise, for each day of the week. The only thing that changes is the time of sunrise, so all you have to do is check the sunrise time on any given day of the year, and go by the lucky hours listed for that time and day. For this reason, it doesn't matter if it's standard or daylight savings time. It also doesn't matter if you are at home or in another part of the world. Just go by the sunrise time for the location you are in, to determine your lucky hours.

Refer to *Sample Chart* on page *36* for instructions.

GEMINI PERSONAL

SUNRISE	SUNDAY	MONDAY	TUESDAY
3:00 AM **to** **3:29 AM**	4:00 AM - 7:00 AM 11:00 AM - 2:00 PM 6:00 PM - 9:00 PM 1:00 AM - 4:00 AM	8:00 AM - 11:00 AM 3:00 PM - 6:00 PM 10:00 PM - 1:00 AM	5:00 AM - 8:00 AM 12:00 PM - 3:00 PM 7:00 PM - 10:00 PM
3:30 AM **to** **3:59 AM**	4:30 AM - 7:30 AM 11:30 AM - 2:30 PM 6:30 PM - 9:30 PM 1:30 AM - 4:30 AM	8:30 AM - 11:30 AM 3:30 PM - 6:30 PM 10:30 PM - 1:30 AM	5:30 AM - 8:30 AM 12:30 PM - 3:30 PM 7:30 PM - 10:30 PM
4:00 AM **to** **4:29 AM**	5:00 AM - 8:00 AM 12:00 PM - 3:00 PM 7:00 PM - 10:00 PM 2:00 AM - 5:00 AM	9:00 AM - 12:00 PM 4:00 PM - 7:00 PM 11:00 PM - 2:00 AM	6:00 AM - 9:00 AM 1:00 PM - 4:00 PM 8:00 PM - 11:00 PM
4:30 AM **to** **4:59 AM**	5:30 AM - 8:30 AM 12:30 PM - 3:30 PM 7:30 PM - 10:30 PM 2:30 AM - 5:30 AM	9:30 AM - 12:30 PM 4:30 PM - 7:30 PM 11:30 PM - 2:30 AM	6:30 AM - 9:30 AM 1:30 PM - 4:30 PM 8:30 PM - 11:30 PM
5:00 AM **to** **5:29 AM**	6:00 AM - 9:00 AM 1:00 PM - 4:00 PM 8:00 PM - 11:00 PM 3:00 AM - 6:00 AM	10:00 AM - 1:00 PM 5:00 PM - 8:00 PM 12:00 AM - 3:00 AM	7:00 AM -10:00 AM 2:00 PM - 5:00 PM 9:00 PM - 12:00 AM
5:30 AM **to** **5:59 AM**	6:30 AM - 9:30 AM 1:30 PM - 4:30 PM 8:30 PM - 11:30 PM 3:30 AM - 6:30 AM	10:30 AM - 1:30 PM 5:30 PM - 8:30 PM 12:30 AM - 3:30 AM	7:30 AM -10:30 AM 2:30 PM - 5:30 PM 9:30 PM - 12:30 AM

Refer to *Sample Chart* on page *36* for instructions.

LUCK CHART

WEDNESDAY	THURSDAY	FRIDAY	SATURDAY
2:00 AM - 5:00 AM 9:00 AM - 12:00 PM 4:00 PM - 7:00 PM 11:00 PM - 2:00 AM	6:00 AM - 9:00 AM 1:00 PM - 4:00 PM 8:00 PM - 11:00 PM	3:00 AM - 6:00 AM 10:00 AM - 1:00 PM 5:00 PM - 8:00 PM 12:00 AM - 3:00 AM	7:00 AM - 10:00 AM 2:00 PM - 5:00 PM 9:00 PM -12:00 AM
2:30 AM - 5:30 AM 9:30 AM - 12:30 PM 4:30 PM - 7:30 PM 11:30 PM - 2:30 AM	6:30 AM - 9:30 AM 1:30 PM - 4:30 PM 8:30 PM - 11:30 PM	3:30 AM - 6:30 AM 10:30 AM - 1:30 PM 5:30 PM - 8:30 PM 12:30 AM - 3:30 AM	7:30 AM - 10:30 AM 2:30 PM - 5:30 PM 9:30 PM - 12:30 AM
3:30 AM - 6:00 AM 10:00 AM - 1:00 PM 5:00 PM - 8:00 PM 12:00 AM - 3:00 AM	7:00 AM - 10:00 AM 2:00 PM - 5:00 PM 9:00 PM - 12:00 AM	4:00 AM - 7:00 AM 11:00 AM - 2:00 PM 6:00 PM - 9:00 PM 1:00 AM - 4:00 AM	8:00 AM - 11:00 AM 3:00 PM - 6:00 PM 10:00 PM - 1:00 AM
3:30 AM - 6:30 AM 10:30 AM - 1:30 PM 5:30 PM - 8:30 PM 12:30 AM - 3:30 AM	7:30 AM - 10:30 AM 2:30 PM - 5:30 PM 9:30 PM - 12:30 AM	4:30 AM - 7:30 AM 11:30 AM - 2:30 PM 6:30 PM - 9:30 PM 1:30 AM - 4:30 AM	8:30 AM -11:30 AM 3:30 PM - 6:30 PM 10:30 PM - 1:30 AM
4:00 AM - 7:00 AM 11:00 AM - 2:00 PM 6:00 PM - 9:00 PM 1:00 AM - 4:00 AM	8:00 AM - 11:00 AM 3:00 PM - 6:00 PM 10:00 PM - 1:00 AM	5:00 AM - 8:00 AM 12:00 PM - 3:00 PM 7:00 PM - 10:00 PM 2:00 AM - 5:00 AM	9:00 AM -12:00 PM 4:00 PM - 7:00 PM 11:00 PM - 2:00 AM
4:30 AM - 7:30 AM 11:30 AM - 2:30 PM 6:30 PM - 9:30 PM 1:30 AM - 4:30 AM	8:30 AM - 11:30 AM 3:30 PM - 6:30 PM 10:30 PM - 1:30 AM	5:30 AM - 8:30 AM 12:30 PM - 3:30 PM 7:30 PM - 10:30 PM 2:30 AM - 5:30 AM	9:30 AM -12:30 PM 4:30 PM - 7:30 PM 11:30 PM - 2:30 AM

SUNRISE	SUNDAY	MONDAY	TUESDAY
6:00 AM **to** **6:29 AM**	7:00 AM - 10:00 AM 2:00 PM - 5:00 PM 9:00 PM - 12:00 AM 4:00 AM - 7:00 AM	11:00 AM - 2:00 PM 6:00 PM - 9:00 PM 1:00 AM - 4:00 AM	8:00 AM - 11:00 AM 3:00 PM - 6:00 PM 10:00 PM - 1:00 AM
6:30 AM **to** **6:59 AM**	7:30 AM - 10:30 AM 2:30 PM - 5:30 PM 9:30 PM - 12:30 AM 4:30 AM - 7:30 AM	11:30 AM - 2:30 PM 6:30 PM - 9:30 PM 1:30 AM - 4:30 AM	8:30 AM - 11:30 AM 3:30 PM - 6:30 PM 10:30 PM - 1:30 AM
7:00 AM **to** **7:29 AM**	8:00 AM - 11:00 AM 3:00 PM - 6:00 PM 10:00 PM - 1:00 AM	4:00 AM - 7:00 AM 12:00 PM - 3:00 PM 7:00 PM - 10:00 PM 2:00 AM - 5:00 AM	9:00 AM - 12:00 PM 4:00 PM - 7:00 PM 11:00 PM - 2:00 AM
7:30 AM **to** **7:59 AM**	8:30 AM - 11:30 AM 3:30 PM - 6:30 PM 10:30 PM - 1:30 AM	4:30 AM - 7:30 AM 12:30 PM - 3:30 PM 7:30 PM - 10:30 PM 2:30 AM - 5:30 AM	9:30 AM - 12:30 PM 4:30 PM - 7:30 PM 11:30 PM - 2:30 AM
8:00 AM **to** **8:29 AM**	9:00 AM - 12:00 PM 4:00 PM - 7:00 PM 11:00 PM - 2:00 AM	5:00 AM - 8:00 AM 1:00 PM - 4:00 PM 8:00 PM - 11:00 PM 3:00 AM - 6:00 AM	10:00 AM -1:00 PM 5:00 PM - 8:00 PM 12:00 AM - 3:00 AM
8:30 AM **to** **8:59 AM**	9:30 AM - 12:30 PM 4:30 PM - 7:30 PM 11:30 PM - 2:30 AM	5:30 AM - 8:30 AM 1:30 PM - 4:30 PM 8:30 PM - 11:30 PM 3:30 AM - 6:30 AM	10:30 AM -1:30 PM 5:30 PM - 8:30 PM 12:30 AM - 3:30 AM

WEDNESDAY	THURSDAY	FRIDAY	SATURDAY
5:00 AM - 8:00 AM 12:00 AM - 3:00 PM 7:00 PM - 10:00 PM 2:00 AM - 5:00 AM	9:00 AM - 12:00 PM 4:00 PM -7:00 PM 11:00 PM - 2:00 AM	6:00 AM -9:00 AM 1:00 PM - 4:00 PM 8:00 PM -11:00 PM 3:00 AM - 6:00 AM	10:00 AM - 1:00 PM 5:00 PM - 8:00 PM 12:00 AM -3:00 AM
5:30 AM - 8:30 AM 12:30 PM - 3:30 PM 7:30 PM - 10:30 PM 2:30 AM - 5:30 AM	9:30 AM - 12:30 PM 4:30 PM - 7:30 PM 11:30 PM - 2:30 AM	6:30 AM - 9:30 AM 1:30 PM - 4:30 PM 8:30 PM - 11:30 PM 3:30 AM - 6:30 AM	10:30 AM - 1:30 PM 5:30 PM - 8:30 PM 12:30 AM - 3:30 AM
6:00 AM - 9:00 AM 1:00 PM - 4:00 PM 8:00 PM - 11:00 PM 3:00 AM - 6:00 AM	10:00 AM - 1:00 PM 5:00 PM - 8:00 PM 12:00 AM - 3:00 AM	7:00 AM - 10:00 AM 2:00 PM - 5:00 PM 9:00 PM - 12:00 AM 4:00 AM - 7:00 AM	11:00 AM - 2:00 PM 6:00 PM - 9:00 PM 1:00 AM - 4:00 AM
6:30 AM - 9:30 AM 1:30 PM - 4:30 PM 8:30 PM - 11:30 PM 3:30 AM - 6:30 AM	10:30 AM - 1:30 PM 5:30 PM - 8:30 PM 12:30 AM - 3:30 AM	7:30 AM - 10:30 AM 2:30 PM - 5:30 PM 9:30 PM - 12:30 AM 4:30 AM - 7:30 AM	11:30 AM - 2:30 PM 6:30 PM - 9:30 PM 1:30 AM - 4:30 AM
7:00 AM - 10:00 AM 2:00 PM - 5:00 PM 9:00 PM - 12:00 AM 4:00 AM - 7:00 AM	11:00 AM - 2:00 PM 6:00 PM - 9:00 PM 1:00 AM - 4:00 AM	8:00 AM - 11:00 AM 3:00 PM - 6:00 PM 10:00 PM - 1:00 AM 5:00 AM - 8:00 AM	12:00 PM -3:00 PM 7:00 PM - 10:00 PM 2:00 AM - 5:00 AM
7:30 AM - 10:30 AM 2:30 AM - 5:30 PM 9:30 PM - 12:30 AM 4:30 AM - 7:30 AM	11:30 AM - 2:30 PM 6:30 PM - 9:30 PM 1:30 AM - 4:30 AM	8:30 AM - 11:30 AM 3:30 PM - 6:30 PM 10:30 PM - 1:30 AM 5:30 AM - 8:30 AM	12:30 PM -3:30 PM 7:30 PM - 10:30 PM 2:30 AM - 5:30 AM

CANCER

There is no getting away from the fact, that there are only nine numbers by which all our calculations on this earth are made. Beyond these nine numbers, all the rest are repetition, as 10 is a 1 with a 0 added, eleven (11) is 1+1=2; and so on. Every number, no matter how high, can be reduced to a single figure. That is why your lucky numbers first appear as single numbers, followed by numbers adding up to this single number, up to 31. However, any number over 31 which adds up to any of your single lucky numbers, is also lucky for you.

Your first lucky number is - 2 - and all numbers adding up to 2, such as 11-20-29 - Lucky day Sunday. This number was determined by combining your celestial number with other factors of your sun sign.

Your luckiest number is 2. Bear this in mind at all times. When you buy a ticket of any sort, make sure that the serial number has the predominant number 2 in it, and buy it during one of your lucky periods. Also a street address containing one or more 2's; horse number 2, player number 2 in a game; a 2 rolled in dice; room number 2 in a hotel/motel; and so on. These are all considered fortunate for you. You can also combine number 2 with your other lucky numbers.

Your second lucky number is your birth date.

Your third lucky numbers are - 2 and 7 - as well as 16 and 25 - Lucky days are Monday and Sunday. These are the numbers assigned to the Moon, ruling planet of Cancer.

NOTE: Since 2 and 7 add up to 9, you will have a certain degree of luck with the 3-6-9 combination such as; 3-12-21-30 (lucky day Thursday); 6-15-24 (lucky day Friday); 9-18-27 (lucky day Tuesday). All these numbers are especially lucky if they fall on Tuesday, Thursday or Friday.

SPECIAL NOTE: Persons born under the sign of Cancer, are probably the luckiest people of the Zodiac, because they have the most lucky numbers and lucky days. The numbers 2 and 7 are interrelated to 1-10-19-28 and 4-13-22-31 (lucky day Sunday). Therefore, all these numbers are especially lucky if they fall on Monday or Sunday.

If your birth date is one of the above dates, that number and its series will be extremely lucky for you.

BIRTH DATES

NUMBERS: 1 - 10 - 19 - 28
LUCKY DAYS: Sunday and Monday.

People born on one of these dates are fortunate, because they are related to 4-13-22-31 (lucky day Sunday), and the series of 1 and 4 are interrelated to 2-11-20-29 and 7-16-25 (lucky day Monday). Therefore, all these numbers are especially lucky on Sunday and Monday.

Your lucky yearly periods are; July 20th to August 28th and March 21st to April 28th.

NUMBERS: 2 - 11 - 20 - 29
LUCKY DAYS: Monday and Sunday.

If one of these dates is your birth date, these numbers are extremely lucky for you, since they happen to be the same as your first and third lucky numbers.

People born on one of these dates are fortunate, because these numbers are related to 7-16-25 (lucky day Monday), and the series of 2 and 7 are interrelated to 1-10-19-28 and 4-13-22-31 (lucky day Sunday). Therefore, all these numbers are especially lucky on Monday and Sunday.

Your lucky yearly period is from June 21st to July 27th.

NUMBERS: 3 - 12 - 21 - 30
LUCKY DAY: Thursday

NOTE: Since these numbers are part of the 3-6-9 combination, you will have a certain degree of luck with 6-15-24 (lucky day Friday) and 9-18-27 (lucky day Tuesday). All these numbers are especially lucky on Thursday, Tuesday and Friday.

Your lucky yearly periods are; February 19th to March 27th and November 21st to December 27th.

NUMBERS: 4 - 13 - 22 - 31
LUCKY DAYS: Sunday and Monday.

People born on one of these dates are fortunate, because these numbers are related to 1-10-19-28 (lucky day Sunday), and the series of 4 and 1 are interrelated to 2-11-20-29 and 7-16-25 (lucky day Monday). Therefore, all these numbers are especially lucky on Sunday and Monday.

Your lucky yearly period is from June 21st to August 30th.

NUMBERS: 5 - 14 - 23
LUCKY DAY: Wednesday

You will also have a certain degree of luck on Fridays.

Your lucky yearly periods are; May 21st to June 27th and August 21st to September 27th.

NUMBERS: 6 - 15 - 24
LUCKY DAY: Friday

NOTE: Since these numbers are part of the 3-6-9 combination, you will have a certain degree of luck with 3-12-21-30 (lucky day Thursday) and 9-18-27 (lucky day

Tuesday). All these numbers are especially lucky on Friday, Tuesday and Thursday.

Your lucky yearly periods are; April 20th to May 27th and September 21st to October 27th.

NUMBERS: 7 - 16 - 25
LUCKY DAYS: Monday and Sunday.

If your birth date falls on one of these dates, these numbers are extremely fortunate for you, since they happen to be the same as your third lucky number.

People born on one of these dates are fortunate, because these numbers are related to 2-11-20-29 (lucky day Monday), and the series of 7 and 2 are interrelated to 1-10-19-28 and 4-13-22-31 (lucky day Sunday). Therefore, all these numbers are especially lucky on Monday and Sunday.

Your lucky yearly period is from June 21st to July 27th, and less strongly from this date to the end of August.

NUMBERS: 8 - 17 - 26
LUCKY DAY: Saturday

Since number 8 has a connection to number 4, you could have a certain degree of luck on Sundays.

Your lucky yearly periods are; from December 21st to December 31st, all of January up to February 26th.

NUMBERS: 9 - 18 - 27
LUCKY DAY: Tuesday

NOTE: Since these numbers are part of the 3-6-9 combination, you will have a certain degree of luck with 3-12-21-30 (lucky day Thursday) and 6-15-24 (lucky day Friday). All these numbers are especially lucky on Tuesday, Thursday and Friday.

Your lucky yearly periods are; March 21st to April 27th and October 21st to November 27th.

DECANS

Note: Decans are Stars or Constellations that rise once every ten days and by which the ancient Egyptians used to tell time.

There are certain periods during the year that are most fortunate for you, when your chances of winning are amplified even more.

If you were born on June 22, 23, 24, 25, 26, 27, 28, 29, 30 and July 1 and 2 - the following periods are lucky for you.

February 20th to 29th

April 21st to May 1st

August 24th to September 3rd

October 24th to November 2nd

If you were born on June 3, 4, 5, 6, 7, 8, 9, 10, 11, 12, 13 - the following periods are lucky for you.

March 1st to 10th

May 2nd to 12th

September 4th to 13th

November 3rd to 12th

If you were born on June 14, 15, 16, 17, 18, 19, 20, 21, 22, 23 - the following periods are lucky for you.

March 11th to 20th

May 12th to 21st

September 14th to 23rd

November 13th to 22nd

The lucky periods in your Personal Luck Chart, and your lucky numbers, remain the same for the rest of your life. They are based on your birth date and the time of sunrise, which varies greatly throughout the year. I have provided you with sunrise times from 3:00 a.m. to 9:00 a.m. Your lucky hours have been indicated for each hour of sunrise, for each day of the week. The only thing that changes is the time of sunrise, so all you have to do is check the sunrise time on any given day of the year, and go by the lucky hours listed for that time and day. For this reason, it doesn't matter if it's standard or daylight savings time. It also doesn't matter if you are at home or in another part of the world. Just go by the sunrise time for the location you are in, to determine your lucky hours.

Refer to *Sample Chart* on page *36* for instructions.

CANCER PERSONAL

SUNRISE	SUNDAY	MONDAY	TUESDAY
3:00 AM to **3:29 AM**	5:00 AM - 8:00 AM 12:00 PM - 3:00 PM 7:00 PM - 10:00 PM	2:00 AM - 5:00 AM 9:00 AM - 12:00 PM 4:00 PM - 7:00 PM 11:00 PM - 2:00 AM	6:00 AM - 9:00 AM 1:00 PM - 4:00 PM 8:00 PM - 11:00 PM
3:30 AM to **3:59 AM**	5:30 AM - 8:30 AM 12:30 PM - 3:30 PM 7:30 PM - 10:30 PM	2:30 AM - 5:30 AM 9:30 AM - 12:30 PM 4:30 PM - 7:30 PM 11:30 PM - 2:30 AM	6:30 AM - 9:30 AM 1:30 PM - 4:30 PM 8:30 PM - 11:30 PM
4:00 AM to **4:29 AM**	6:00 AM - 9:00 AM 1:00 PM - 4:00 PM 8:00 PM - 11:00 PM	3:00 AM - 6:00 AM 10:00 AM - 1:00 PM 5:00 PM - 8:00 PM 12:00 AM - 3:00 AM	7:00 AM - 10:00 AM 2:00 PM - 5:00 PM 9:00 PM - 12:00 AM
4:30 AM to **4:59 AM**	6:30 AM - 9:30 AM 1:30 PM - 4:30 PM 8:30 PM - 11:30 PM	3:30 AM - 6:30 AM 10:30 AM - 1:30 PM 5:30 PM - 8:30 PM 12:30 AM - 3:30 AM	7:30 AM - 10:30 AM 2:30 PM - 5:30 PM 9:30 PM - 12:30 AM
5:00 AM to **5:29 AM**	7:00 AM - 10:00 AM 2:00 PM - 5:00 PM 9:00 PM - 12:00 AM	4:00 AM -7:00 AM 11:00 AM - 2:00 PM 6:00 PM - 9:00 PM 1:00 AM - 4:00 AM	8:00 AM - 11:00 AM 3:00 PM - 6:00 PM 10:00 PM - 1:00 AM
5:30 AM to **5:59 AM**	7:30 AM - 10:30 AM 2:30 PM - 5:30 PM 9:30 PM - 12:30 AM	4:30 AM -7:30 AM 11:30 AM - 2:30 PM 6:30 PM - 9:30 PM 1:30 AM - 4:30 AM	8:30 AM - 11:30 AM 3:30 PM - 6:30 PM 10:30 PM - 1:30 AM

Refer to *Sample Chart* on page *36* for instructions.

LUCK CHART

WEDNESDAY	THURSDAY	FRIDAY	SATURDAY
3:00 AM - 6:00 AM 10:00 AM - 1:00 PM 5:00 PM - 8:00 PM 12:00 AM - 3:00 AM	7:00 AM - 10:00 AM 2:00 PM - 5:00 PM 9:00 PM - 12:00 AM	4:00 AM - 7:00 AM 11:00 AM - 2:00 PM 6:00 PM - 9:00 PM 1:00 AM - 4:00 AM	8:00 AM - 11:00 AM 3:00 PM - 6:00 PM 10:00 PM - 1:00 AM
3:30 AM - 6:30 AM 10:30 AM - 1:30 PM 5:30 PM - 8:30 PM 12:30 AM - 3:30 AM	7:30 AM - 10:30 AM 2:30 PM - 5:30 PM 9:30 PM - 12:30 AM	4:30 AM - 7:30 AM 11:30 AM - 2:30 PM 6:30 PM - 9:30 PM 1:30 AM - 4:30 AM	8:30 AM - 11:30 AM 3:30 PM - 6:30 PM 10:30 PM - 1:30 AM
4:00 AM - 7:00 AM 11:00 AM - 2:00 PM 6:00 PM - 9:00 PM 1:00 AM - 4:00 AM	8:00 AM - 11:00 AM 3:00 PM - 6:00 PM 10:00 PM - 1:00 AM	5:00 AM - 8:00 AM 12:00 PM - 3:00 PM 7:00 PM - 10:00 PM 2:00 AM - 5:00 AM	9:00 AM - 12:00 AM 4:00 PM - 7:00 PM 11:00 PM - 2:00 AM
4:30 AM - 7:30 AM 11:30 AM - 2:30 PM 6:30 PM - 9:30 PM 1:30 AM - 4:30 AM	8:30 AM - 11:30 AM 3:30 PM - 6:30 PM 10:30 PM - 1:30 AM	5:30 AM - 8:30 AM 12:30 PM - 3:30 PM 7:30 PM - 10:30 PM 2:30 AM - 5:30 AM	9:30 AM - 12:30 PM 4:30 PM - 7:30 PM 11:30 PM - 2:30 AM
5:00 AM - 8:00 AM 12:00 PM - 3:00 PM 7:00 PM - 10:00 PM 2:00 AM - 5:00 AM	9:00 AM - 12:00 PM 4:00 PM - 7:00 PM 11:00 PM - 2:00 AM	6:00 AM - 9:00 AM 1:00 PM - 4:00 PM 8:00 PM - 11:00 PM 3:00 AM - 6:00 AM	10:00 AM - 1:00 PM 5:00 PM - 8:00 PM 12:00 PM - 3:00 AM
5:30 AM - 8:30 AM 12:30 PM - 3:30 PM 7:30 PM - 10:30 PM 2:30 AM - 5:30 AM	9:30 AM - 12:30 PM 4:30 PM - 7:30 PM 11:30 PM - 2:30 AM	6:30 AM -9:30 AM 1:30 PM - 4:30 PM 8:30 PM - 11:30 PM 3:30 AM - 6:30 AM	10:30 AM - 1:30 PM 5:30 PM - 8:30 PM 12:30 AM - 3:30 AM

SUNRISE	SUNDAY	MONDAY	TUESDAY
6:00 AM to **6:29 AM**	8:00 AM - 11:00 AM 3:00 PM - 6:00 PM 10:00 PM - 1:00 AM	5:00 AM - 8:00 AM 12:00 PM - 3:00 PM 7:00 PM - 10:00 PM 2:00 AM - 5:00 AM	9:00 AM -12:00 PM 4:00 PM - 7:00 PM 11:00 PM - 2:00 AM
6:30 AM to **6:59 AM**	8:30 AM - 11:30 AM 3:30 PM - 6:30 PM 10:30 PM - 1:30 AM	5:30 AM - 8:30 AM 12:30 PM - 3:30 PM 7:30 PM - 10:30 PM 2:30 AM - 5:30 AM	9:30 AM - 12:30 PM 4:30 PM - 7:30 PM 11:30 PM - 2:30 AM
7:00 AM to **7:29 AM**	9:00 AM - 12:00 PM 4:00 PM - 7:00 PM 11:00 PM - 2:00 AM	6:00 AM - 9:00 AM 1:00 PM - 4:00 PM 8:00 PM - 11:00 PM 3:00 AM - 6:00 AM	10:00 AM - 1:00 PM 5:00 PM - 8:00 PM 12:00 AM - 3:00 AM
7:30 AM to **7:59 AM**	9:30 AM - 12:30 PM 4:30 PM - 7:30 PM 11:30 PM - 2:30 AM	6:30 AM - 9:30 AM 1:30 PM - 4:30 PM 8:30 PM - 11:30 PM 3:30 AM - 6:30 AM	10:30 AM - 1:30 PM 5:30 PM - 8:30 PM 12:30 AM - 3:30 AM
8:00 AM to **8:29 AM**	10:00 AM -1:00 PM 5:00 PM - 8:00 PM 12:00 AM - 3:00 AM	7:00 AM - 10:00 AM 2:00 PM - 5:00 PM 9:00 PM - 12:00 AM 4:00 AM - 7:00 AM	11:00 AM - 2:00 PM 6:00 PM - 9:00 PM 1:00 AM - 4:00 AM
8:30 AM to **8:59 AM**	10:30 AM -1:30 PM 5:30 PM - 8:30 PM 12:30 AM - 3:30 AM	7:30 AM - 10:30 AM 2:30 PM - 5:30 PM 9:30 PM - 12:30 AM 4:30 AM - 7:30 AM	11:30 AM - 2:30 PM 6:30 PM - 9:30 PM 1:30 AM - 4:30 AM

WEDNESDAY	THURSDAY	FRIDAY	SATURDAY
6:00 AM -9:00 AM 1:00 PM - 4:00 PM 8:00 PM -11:00 PM 3:00 AM - 6:00 AM	10:00 AM - 1:00 PM 5:00 PM - 8:00 PM 12:00 AM -3:00 AM	7:00 AM - 10:00 AM 2:00 PM - 5:00 PM 9:00 PM - 12:00 AM 4:00 AM - 7:00 AM	11:00 AM - 2:00 PM 6:00 PM - 9:00 PM 1:00 AM - 4:00 AM
6:30 AM - 9:30 AM 1:30 PM - 4:30 PM 8:30 PM - 11:30 PM 3:30 AM - 6:30 AM	10:30 AM - 1:30 PM 5:30 PM - 8:30 PM 12:30 AM - 3:30 AM	7:30 AM - 10:30 AM 2:30 PM - 5:30 PM 9:30 PM - 12:30 AM 4:30 AM - 7:30 AM	11:30 AM - 2:30 PM 6:30 PM - 9:30 PM 1:30 AM - 4:30 AM
7:00 AM - 10:00 AM 2:00 PM - 5:00 PM 9:00 PM - 12:00 AM 4:00 AM -7:00 AM	11:00 AM - 2:00 PM 6:00 PM - 9:00 PM 1:00 AM - 4:00 AM	8:00 AM - 11:00 AM 3:00 PM - 6:00 PM 10:00 PM - 1:00 AM 5:00 AM - 8:00 AM	12:00 PM - 3:00 PM 7:00 PM - 10:00 PM 2:00 AM - 5:00 AM
7:30 AM - 10:30 AM 2:30 PM - 5:30 PM 9:30 PM - 12:30 AM 4:30 AM - 7:30 AM	11:30 AM - 2:30 PM 6:30 PM - 9:30 PM 1:30 AM - 4:30 AM	8:30 AM - 11:30 AM 3:30 PM - 6:30 PM 10:30 PM - 1:30 AM 5:30 AM - 8:30 AM	12:30 PM - 3:30 PM 7:30 PM - 10:30 PM 2:30 AM - 5:30 AM
8:00 AM - 11:00 AM 3:00 PM - 6:00 PM 10:00 PM - 1:00 AM 5:00 AM - 8:00 AM	12:00 AM - 3:00 PM 7:00 PM - 10:00 PM 2:00 AM - 5:00 AM	9:00 AM - 12:00 PM 4:00 PM - 7:00 PM 11:00 PM - 2:00 AM	6:00 AM - 9:00 AM 1:00 PM - 4:00 PM 8:00 PM -11:00 PM 3:00 AM - 6:00 AM
8:30 AM - 11:30 AM 3:30 PM - 6:30 PM 10:30 PM - 1:30 AM 5:30 AM - 8:30 AM	12:30 PM - 3:30 PM 7:30 PM - 10:30 PM 2:30 AM - 5:30 AM	9:30 AM - 12:30 PM 4:30 PM - 7:30 PM 11:30 PM - 2:30 AM	6:30 AM - 9:30 AM 1:30 PM - 4:30 PM 8:30 PM - 11:30 PM 3:30 AM - 6:30 AM

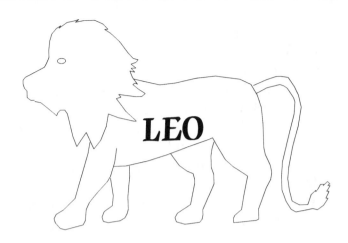

LEO

There is no getting away from the fact, that there are only nine numbers by which all our calculations on this earth are made. Beyond these nine numbers, all the rest are repetition, as 10 is a 1 with a 0 added, and eleven (11) is 1+1=2; and so on. Every number, no matter how high, can be reduced to a single figure. This is why your lucky numbers first appear as single numbers, followed by numbers adding up to this single number, up to 31. However, any number over 31 which adds up to any of your single lucky numbers, is also lucky for you.

Your first lucky number is - 5 - and all numbers adding up to 5, such as 14 and 23 - Lucky day Sunday. This number was determined by combining your celestial number with other factors of your sun sign.

Your luckiest number is 5. Bear this in mind at all times. When you buy a ticket of any sort, make sure that the serial number has the predominant number 5 in it, and buy it during one of your lucky periods. Also a street address containing one or more 5's; horse number 5, player number 5 in a game; a 5 rolled in dice; room number 5 in a hotel/motel; and so on. These are all considered fortunate for you. You can also combine number 5 with your other lucky numbers.

Your second lucky number is your birth date.

Your third lucky numbers are - 1 and 4 - as well as 10-19-28 and 13-22-31- Lucky day Sunday. These are the numbers assigned to the Sun, ruling planet of Leo.

NOTE: You are fortunate, because numbers 1 and 4 are interrelated to 2-11-20-29 and
7-16-25 (Lucky day Monday). Therefore, all these numbers are lucky for you, especially if they fall on Sunday or Monday.

BIRTH DATES

NUMBERS: 1 - 10 - 19 - 28
LUCKY DAYS: Sunday and Monday

If one of these dates is your birth date, these numbers are extremely lucky for you, since they happen to be the same as your third lucky number.

People born on one of these dates are fortunate, because these numbers are related to 4-13-22-31 (lucky day Sunday) and the series of 1 and 4 are interrelated to 2-11-20-29 and 7-16-25 (lucky day Monday). Therefore, all these numbers are especially lucky on Sunday and Monday.

Your lucky yearly periods are; July 20th to August 28th and March 21st to April 28th.

NUMBERS: 2 - 11 - 20 - 29
LUCKY DAYS: Monday and Sunday

People born on one of these dates are fortunate, because these numbers are related to 7-16-25 (lucky day Monday), and the series of 2 and 7 are interrelated to 1-10-19-28 and 4-13-22-31 (lucky day Sunday). Therefore, all these numbers are especially lucky on Monday and Sunday.

Your lucky yearly period is from June 21st to July 27th.

NUMBERS: 3 - 12 - 21 - 30
LUCKY DAY: Thursday
NOTE: Since these numbers are part of the 3-6-9 combination, you will have a certain degree of luck with 6-15-24 (lucky day Friday) and 9-18-27 (lucky day Tuesday). All these numbers are especially lucky on Thursday, Tuesday and Friday.

Your lucky yearly periods are; February 19th to March 27th and November 21st to December 27th.

NUMBERS: 4 - 13 - 22 - 31
LUCKY DAYS: Sunday and Monday
If one of these dates is your birth date, these numbers are extremely lucky for you, since they happen to be the same as your third lucky number.

People born on one of these dates are fortunate, because these numbers are related to 1-10-19-28 (lucky day Sunday), and the series of 4 and 1 are interrelated to 2-11-20-29 and 7-16-25 (lucky day Monday). Therefore, all these numbers are especially lucky on Sunday and Monday.

Your lucky yearly period is from June 21st to August 30th.

NUMBERS: 5 - 14 - 23
LUCKY DAY: Wednesday
If one of these dates is your birth date, these numbers are extremely lucky for you, since they happen to be the same as your first lucky number. You will also have a certain degree of luck on Fridays.

Your lucky yearly periods are; May 21st to June 27th and August 21st to September 27th.

NUMBERS: 6 - 15 - 24
LUCKY DAY: Friday
NOTE: Since these numbers are part of the 3-6-9 combination, you will have a certain degree of luck with 3-12-21-30 (lucky day Thursday) and 9-18-27 (lucky day Tuesday). All these numbers are especially lucky on Friday, Tuesday and Thursday.

Your lucky yearly periods are; April 20th to May 27th and September 21st to October 27th.

NUMBERS: 7 - 16 - 25

LUCKY DAYS: Monday and Sunday.

People born on one of these dates are fortunate, because these numbers are related to 2-11-20-29 (lucky day Monday), and the series of 7 and 2 are interrelated to 1-10-19-28 and 4-13-22-31 (lucky day Sunday). Therefore, all these numbers are especially lucky on Monday and Sunday.

Your lucky yearly period is from June 21st to July 27th, and less strongly from this date to the end of August.

NUMBERS: 8 - 17 - 26

LUCKY DAY: Saturday

Since number 8 has a connection to number 4, you could have a certain degree of luck on Sundays.

Your lucky yearly periods are; from December 21st to December 31st, all of January up to February 26th.

NUMBER: 9 - 18 - 27

LUCKY DAY: Tuesday

NOTE: Since these numbers are part of the 3-6-9 combination, you will have a certain degree of luck with 3-12-21-30 (lucky day Thursday) and 6-15-24 (lucky day Friday). All these numbers are especially lucky on Tuesday, Thursday and Friday.

Your lucky yearly periods are; March 21st to April 27th and October 21st to November 27th.

DECANS

Note: Decans are Stars or Constellations that rise once every ten days and by which the ancient Egyptians used to tell time.

There are certain periods during the year that are most fortunate for you, when your chances of winning are amplified even more.

If you were born on July 24, 25, 26, 27, 28, 29, 30, 31 and August 1, 2, 3 - the following periods are lucky for you.

> March 21st to 31st
> May 22nd to June 1st
> September 24th to October 3rd
> November 23rd to December 2nd

If you were born on August 4, 5, 6, 7, 8, 9, 10, 11, 12, 13 - the following periods are lucky for you.

> April 1st to 11th
> June 2nd to 12th
> October 3rd to 13th
> December 3rd to 12th

If you were born on August 14, 15, 16, 17, 18, 19, 20, 21, 22, 23 - the following periods are lucky for you.

> April 10th to 20th
> June 12th to 21st
> October 13th to 23rd
> December 12th to 2nd

The lucky periods in your Personal Luck Chart, and your lucky numbers, remain the same for the rest of your life. They are based on your birth date and the time of sunrise, which varies greatly throughout the year. I have provided you with sunrise times from 3:00 a.m. to 9:00 a.m. Your lucky hours have been indicated for each hour of sunrise, for each day of the week. The only thing that changes is the time of sunrise, so all you have to do is check the sunrise time on any given day of the year, and go by the lucky hours listed for that time and day. For this reason, it doesn't matter if it's standard or daylight savings time. It also doesn't matter if you are at home or in another part of the world. Just go by the sunrise time for the location you are in, to determine your lucky hours.

Refer to *Sample Chart* on page *36* for instructions.

LEO PERSONAL

SUNRISE	SUNDAY	MONDAY	TUESDAY
3:00 AM **to** **3:29 AM**	2:00 AM - 5:00 AM 9:00 AM - 12:00 PM 4:00 PM - 7:00 PM 11:00 PM - 2:00 AM	6:00 AM - 9:00 AM 1:00 PM - 4:00 PM 8:00 PM - 11:00 PM	3:00 AM - 6:00 AM 10:00 AM - 1:00 PM 5:00 PM - 8:00 PM 12:00 AM - 3:00 AM
3:30 AM **to** **3:59 AM**	2:30 AM - 5:30 AM 9:30 AM - 12:30 PM 4:30 PM -7:30 PM 11:30 PM - 2:30 AM	6:30 AM - 9:30 AM 1:30 PM - 4:30 PM 8:30 PM - 11:30 PM	3:30 AM - 6:30 AM 10:30 AM - 1:30 PM 5:30 PM - 8:30 PM 12:30 AM - 3:30 AM
4:00 AM **to** **4:29 AM**	3:00 AM - 6:00 AM 10:00 AM - 1:00 PM 5:00 PM - 8:00 PM 12:00 AM - 3:00 AM	7:00 AM - 10:00 AM 2:00 PM - 5:00 PM 9:00 PM - 12:00 AM	4:00 AM -7:00 AM 11:00 AM - 2:00 PM 6:00 PM - 9:00 PM 1:00 AM - 4:00 AM
4:30 AM **to** **4:59 AM**	3:30 AM - 6:30 AM 10:30 AM - 1:30 PM 5:30 PM - 8:30 PM 12:30 AM - 3:30 AM	7:30 AM - 10:30 AM 2:30 PM - 5:30 PM 9:30 PM - 12:30 AM	4:30 AM -7:30 AM 11:30 AM - 2:30 PM 6:30 PM - 9:30 PM 1:30 AM - 4:30 AM
5:00 AM **to** **5:29 AM**	4:00 AM - 7:00 AM 11:00 AM - 2:00 PM 6:00 PM - 9:00 PM 1:00 AM - 4:00 AM	8:00 AM - 11:00 AM 3:00 PM - 6:00 PM 10:00 PM - 1:00 AM	5:00 AM - 8:00 AM 12:00 PM - 3:00 PM 7:00 PM - 10:00 PM 2:00 AM - 5:00 AM
5:30 AM **to** **5:59 AM**	4:30 AM - 7:30 AM 11:30 AM - 2:30 PM 6:30 PM - 9:30 PM 1:30 AM - 4:30 AM	8:30 AM - 11:30 AM 3:30 PM - 6:30 PM 10:30 PM - 1:30 AM	5:30 AM - 8:30 AM 12:30 PM - 3:30 PM 7:30 PM - 10:30 PM 2:30 AM - 5:30 AM

Refer to **Sample Chart** on page **36** for instructions.

LUCK CHART

WEDNESDAY	THURSDAY	FRIDAY	SATURDAY
7:00 AM - 10:00 AM 2:00 PM - 5:00 PM 9:00 PM - 12:00 AM	4:00 AM - 7:00 AM 11:00 AM - 2:00 PM 6:00 PM - 9:00 PM 1:00 AM - 4:00 AM	8:00 AM - 11:00 AM 3:00 PM - 6:00 PM 10:00 PM - 1:00 AM	5:00 AM - 8:00 AM 12:00 PM - 3:00 PM 7:00 PM - 10:00 PM
7:30 AM - 10:30 AM 2:30 PM - 5:30 PM 9:30 PM - 12:30 AM	4:30 AM - 7:30 AM 11:30 AM - 2:30 PM 6:30 PM - 9:30 PM 1:30 AM - 4:30 AM	8:30 AM - 11:30 AM 3:30 PM - 6:30 PM 10:30 PM - 1:30 AM	5:30 AM - 8:30 AM 12:30 PM - 3:30 PM 7:30 PM - 10:30 PM
8:00 AM - 11:00 AM 3:00 PM - 6:00 PM 10:00 PM - 1:00 AM	5:00 AM - 8:00 AM 12:00 PM - 3:00 PM 7:00 PM - 10:00 PM 2:00 AM - 5:00 AM	9:00 AM - 12:00 PM 4:00 PM - 7:00 PM 11:00 PM - 2:00 AM	6:00 AM - 9:00 AM 1:00 PM - 4:00 PM 8:00 PM - 11:00 PM
8:30 AM - 11:30 AM 3:30 PM - 6:30 PM 10:30 PM - 1:30 AM	5:30 AM - 8:30 AM 12:30 PM - 3:30 PM 7:30 PM - 10:30 PM 2:30 AM - 5:30 AM	9:30 AM - 12:30 PM 4:30 PM - 7:30 PM 11:30 PM - 2:30 PM	6:30 AM -9:30 AM 1:30 PM - 4:30 PM 8:30 PM - 11:30 PM
9:00 AM - 12:00 PM 4:00 PM - 7:00 PM 11:00 PM - 2:00 AM	6:00 AM - 9:00 AM 1:00 PM - 4:00 PM 8:00 PM - 11:00 PM 3:00 AM - 6:00 AM	10:00 AM - 1:00 PM 5:00 PM - 8:00 PM 12:00 PM - 3:00 AM	7:00 AM - 10:00 AM 2:00 PM - 5:00 PM 9:00 PM - 12:00 AM
9:30 AM - 12:30 PM 4:30 PM - 7:30 PM 11:30 PM - 2:30 AM	6:30 AM -9:30 AM 1:30 PM - 4:30 PM 8:30 PM - 11:30 PM 3:30 AM - 6:30 AM	10:30 AM - 1:30 PM 5:30 PM - 8:30 PM 12:30 AM - 3:30 AM	7:30 AM - 10:30 AM 2:30 PM - 5:30 PM 9:30 PM - 12:30 AM

SUNRISE	SUNDAY	MONDAY	TUESDAY
6:00 AM **to** **6:29 AM**	5:00 AM - 8:00 AM 12:00 PM - 3:00 PM 7:00 PM - 10:00 PM 2:00 AM - 5:00 AM	9:00 AM -12:00 PM 4:00 PM - 7:00 PM 11:00 PM - 2:00 AM	6:00 AM - 9:00 AM 1:00 PM - 4:00 PM 8:00 PM - 11:00 PM 3:00 AM - 6:00 AM
6:30 AM **to** **6:59 AM**	5:30 AM - 8:30 AM 12:30 PM - 3:30 PM 7:30 PM - 10:30 PM 2:30 AM - 5:30 AM	9:30 AM - 12:30 PM 4:30 PM - 7:30 PM 11:30 PM - 2:30 AM	6:30 AM - 9:30 AM 1:30 PM - 4:30 PM 8:30 PM - 11:30 PM 3:30 AM - 6:30 AM
7:00 AM **to** **7:29 AM**	6:00 AM - 9:00 AM 1:00 PM - 4:00 PM 8:00 PM - 11:00 PM 3:00 AM - 6:00 AM	10:00 AM -1:00 PM 5:00 PM - 8:00 PM 12:00 AM - 3:00 AM	7:00 AM - 10:00 AM 2:00 PM - 5:00 PM 9:00 PM - 12:00 AM 4:00 AM - 7:00 AM
7:30 AM **to** **7:59 AM**	6:30 AM - 9:30 AM 1:30 PM - 4:30 PM 8:30 PM - 11:30 PM 3:30 AM - 6:30 AM	10:30 AM -1:30 PM 5:30 PM - 8:30 PM 12:30 AM - 3:30 AM	7:30 AM - 10:30 AM 2:30 PM - 5:30 PM 9:30 PM - 12:30 AM 4:30 AM - 7:30 AM
8:00 AM **to** **8:29 AM**	7:00 AM - 10:00 AM 2:00 PM - 5:00 PM 9:00 PM - 12:00 AM 4:00 AM - 7:00 AM	11:00 AM - 2:00 PM 6:00 PM - 9:00 PM 1:00 AM - 4:00 AM	8:00 AM - 11:00 AM 3:00 PM - 6:00 PM 10:00 PM - 1:00 AM
8:30 AM **to** **8:59 AM**	7:30 AM - 10:30 AM 2:30 PM - 5:30 PM 9:30 PM - 12:30 PM 4:30 AM - 7:30 AM	11:30 AM - 2:30 PM 6:30 PM - 9:30 PM 1:30 AM - 4:30 AM	8:30 AM - 11:30 AM 3:30 PM - 6:30 PM 10:30 PM - 1:30 AM

WEDNESDAY	THURSDAY	FRIDAY	SATURDAY
10:00 AM - 1:00 PM 5:00 PM - 8:00 PM 12:00 AM - 3:00 AM	7:00 AM - 10:00 AM 2:00 PM - 5:00 PM 9:00 PM - 12:00 AM 4:00 AM - 7:00 AM	11:00 AM - 2:00 PM 6:00 PM - 9:00 PM 1:00 AM - 4:00 AM	8:00 AM - 11:00 AM 3:00 PM - 6:00 PM 10:00 PM - 1:00 AM
10:30 AM - 1:30 PM 5:30 PM - 8:30 PM 12:30 AM - 3:30 AM	7:30 AM - 10:30 AM 2:30 PM - 5:30 PM 9:30 PM - 12:30 AM 4:30 AM - 7:30 AM	11:30 AM - 2:30 PM 6:30 PM - 9:30 PM 1:30 AM - 4:30 AM	8:30 AM - 11:30 AM 3:30 PM - 6:30 PM 10:30 PM - 1:30 AM
11:00 AM - 2:00 PM 6:00 PM - 9:00 PM 1:00 AM - 4:00 AM	8:00 AM - 11:00 AM 3:00 PM - 6:00 PM 10:00 PM - 1:00 AM 5:00 AM - 8:00 AM	5:00 AM - 8:00 AM 12:00 PM - 3:00 PM 7:00 PM - 10:00 PM 2:00 AM - 5:00 AM	9:00 AM - 12:00 PM 4:00 PM - 7:00 PM 11:00 PM - 2:00 AM
11:30 AM - 2:30 PM 6:30 PM - 9:30 PM 1:30 AM - 4:30 AM	8:30 AM - 11:30 AM 3:30 PM - 6:30 PM 10:30 PM - 1:30 AM 5:30 AM - 8:30 AM	5:30 AM - 8:30 AM 12:30 PM - 3:30 PM 7:30 PM - 10:30 PM 2:30 AM - 5:30 AM	9:30 AM - 12:30 PM 4:30 PM - 7:30 PM 11:30 PM - 2:30 AM
5:00 AM - 8:00 AM 12:00 PM - 3:00 PM 7:00 PM - 10:00 PM 2:00 AM - 5:00 AM	9:00 AM - 12:00 PM 4:00 PM - 7:00 PM 11:00 PM - 2:00 AM 6:00 AM - 9:00 AM	6:00 AM - 9:00 AM 1:00 PM - 4:00 PM 8:00 PM -11:00 PM 3:00 AM - 6:00 AM	10:00 AM - 1:00 PM 5:00 PM - 8:00 PM 12:00 AM - 3:00 AM
5:30 AM - 8:30 AM 12:30 PM - 3:30 PM 7:30 PM - 10:30 PM 2:30 AM - 5:30 AM	9:30 AM - 12:30 PM 4:30 PM - 7:30 PM 11:30 PM - 2:30 AM	6:30 AM - 9:30 AM 1:30 PM - 4:30 PM 8:30 PM - 11:30 PM 3:30 AM - 6:30 AM	10:30 AM - 1:30 PM 5:30 PM - 8:30 PM 12:30 AM - 3:30 AM

VIRGO

There is no getting away from the fact, that there are only nine numbers by which all our calculations on this earth are made. Beyond these nine numbers, all the rest are repetition, as 10 is a 1 with a 0 added, eleven (11) is 1 +1 = 2; and so on. Every number no matter how high, can be reduced to a single figure. This is why your lucky numbers first appear as single numbers, followed by numbers adding up to this single number, up to 31. However, any number over 31 which adds up to any of your single lucky numbers, is also lucky for you.

Your first lucky number is - 3 - and all numbers adding up to 3, such as 12-21-30 - Lucky day Thursday. This number was determined by combining your celestial number with other factors of your sun sign.

Your luckiest number is 3. Bear this is mind at all times. When you buy a ticket of any sort, make sure that the serial number has the predominant number 3 in it, and buy it during one of your lucky periods. Also a street address containing one or more 3's; horse number 3; player number 3 in a game; a 3 rolled in dice; room number 3 in a hotel/motel; and so on. These are all considered fortunate for you. You can also combine number 3 with your other lucky numbers.

Your second lucky number is your birth date.

Your third lucky number is - 5 - as well as 14 and 23 - Lucky day Wednesday. This is the number assigned to the planet Mercury, ruler of Virgo.

BIRTH DATES

NUMBERS: 1 - 10 - 19 - 28
LUCKY DAYS: Sunday and Monday.

People born on one of these dates are fortunate, because these numbers are related to 4-13-22-31 (lucky day Sunday), and the series of 1 and 4 are interrelated to 2-11-20-29 and 7-16-25 (lucky day Monday). Therefore, all these numbers are especially lucky on Sunday and Monday.

Your lucky yearly periods are; July 20th to August 28th and March 21st to April 28th.

NUMBERS: 2 - 11 - 20 - 29
LUCKY DAYS: Monday and Sunday.

People born on one of these dates are fortunate, because these numbers are related to 7-16-25 (lucky day Monday), and the series of 2 and 7 are interrelated to 1-10-19-28 and 4-13-22-31 (lucky day Sunday). Therefore, all these numbers are especially lucky on Monday and Sunday.

Your lucky yearly period is from June 21st to July 27th.

NUMBERS: 3 - 12 - 21 - 30
LUCKY DAY: Thursday

If one of these dates is your birth date, these numbers are extremely lucky for you, since they happen to be the same as your first lucky number.

NOTE: Since these numbers are part of the 3-6-9 combination, you will have a certain degree of luck with 6-15-24 (lucky day Friday) and 9-18-27 (lucky day Tuesday). All these numbers are especially lucky on Thursday, Tuesday and Friday.

Your lucky yearly periods are; February 19th to March 27th and November 21st to December 27th.

NUMBERS: 4 - 13 - 22 - 31
LUCKY DAYS: Sunday and Monday.

People born on one of these dates are fortunate, because these numbers are related to 1-10-19-28 (lucky day Sunday), and the series of 4 and 1 are interrelated to 2-11-20-29 and 7-16-25 (lucky day Monday). Therefore, all these numbers are especially lucky on Sunday and Monday.

Your lucky yearly period is from June 21st to August 30th.

NUMBERS: 5 - 14 - 23
LUCKY DAY: Wednesday

If one of these dates is your birth date, these numbers are extremely lucky for you, since they happen to be the same as your third lucky number. You will also have a certain degree of luck on Fridays.

Your lucky yearly periods are; May 21st to June 27th and August 21st to September 27th.

NUMBERS: 6 - 15 - 24
LUCKY DAY: Friday

NOTE: Since these numbers are part of the 3-6-9 combination, you will have a certain degree of luck with 3-12-21-30 (lucky day Thursday) and 9-18-27 (lucky day Tuesday). All these numbers are especially lucky on Friday, Tuesday and Thursday.

Your lucky yearly periods are; April 20th to May 27th and September 21st to October 27th.

NUMBERS: 7 - 16 - 25
LUCKY DAYS: Monday and Sunday.

People born on one of these dates are fortunate, because these numbers are related to 2-11-20-29 (lucky day Monday), and the series of 7 and 2 are interrelated to 1-10-19-28 and 4-13-22-31 (lucky day Sunday). Therefore, all these numbers are especially lucky on Monday and Sunday.

Your lucky yearly period is from June 21st to July 27th, and less strongly from this date to the end of August.

NUMBERS: 8 - 17 - 26
LUCKY DAY: Saturday

Since number 8 has a connection to number 4, you could have a certain degree of luck on Sundays.

Your lucky yearly periods are; from December 21st to December 31st, all of January up to February 26th.

NUMBERS: 9 - 18 - 27
LUCKY DAY: Tuesday

NOTE: Since these numbers are part of the 3-6-9 combination, you will have a certain degree of luck with 3-12-21-30 (lucky day Thursday) and 6-15-24 (lucky day Friday). All these numbers are especially lucky on Tuesday, Thursday and Friday.

Your lucky yearly periods are; March 21st to April 27th and October 21st to November 27th.

DECANS

Note: Decans are Stars or Constellations that rise once every ten days and by which the ancient Egyptians used to tell time.

There are certain periods during the year that are most fortunate for you, when your chances of winning are amplified even more.

If you were born on August 24, 25, 26, 27, 28, 29, 30, 31 and September 1, 2, 3 - the following periods are lucky for you.

April 21st to May 1st
June 22nd to July 2nd
October 24th to November 3rd
December 22nd to 31st

If you were born on September 4, 5, 6, 7, 8, 9, 10, 11, 12, 13 - the following periods are lucky for you.

January 1st to 11th
May 2nd to 12th
July 3rd to 13th
November 2nd to 12th

If you were born on September 14, 15, 16, 17, 18, 19, 20, 21, 22 - the following periods are lucky for you.

January 11th to 21st
May 11th to 21st
July 12th to 23rd
November 12th to 22nd

The lucky periods in your Personal Luck Chart, and your lucky numbers, remain the same for the rest of your life. They are based on your birth date and the time of sunrise, which varies greatly throughout the year. I have provided you with sunrise times from 3:00 a.m. to 9:00 a.m.. Your lucky hours have been indicated for each hour of sunrise, for each day of the week. The only thing that changes is the time of sunrise, so all you have to do is check the sunrise time on any given day of the year, and go by the lucky hours listed for that time and day. For this reason, it doesn't matter if it's standard or daylight savings time. It also doesn't matter if you are at home or in another part of the world. Just go by the sunrise time for the location you are in, to determine your lucky hours.

Refer to *Sample Chart* on page *36* for instructions.

VIRGO PERSONAL

SUNRISE	SUNDAY	MONDAY	TUESDAY
3:00 AM **to** **3:29 AM**	4:00 AM - 7:00 AM 11:00 AM - 2:00 PM 6:00 PM - 9:00 PM 1:00 AM - 4:00 AM	8:00 AM - 11:00 AM 3:00 PM - 6:00 PM 10:00 PM - 1:00 AM	5:00 AM - 8:00 AM 12:00 PM - 3:00 PM 7:00 PM - 10:00 PM
3:30 AM **to** **3:59 AM**	4:30 AM - 7:30 AM 11:30 AM - 2:30 PM 6:30 PM - 9:30 PM 1:30 AM - 4:30 AM	8:30 AM - 11:30 AM 3:30 PM - 6:30 PM 10:30 PM - 1:30 AM	5:30 AM - 8:30 AM 12:30 PM - 3:30 PM 7:30 PM - 10:30 PM
4:00 AM **to** **4:29 AM**	5:00 AM - 8:00 AM 12:00 PM - 3:00 PM 7:00 PM - 10:00 PM 2:00 AM - 5:00 AM	9:00 AM - 12:00 PM 4:00 PM - 7:00 PM 11:00 PM - 2:00 AM	6:00 AM - 9:00 AM 1:00 PM - 4:00 PM 8:00 PM - 11:00 PM
4:30 AM **to** **4:59 AM**	5:30 AM - 8:30 AM 12:30 PM - 3:30 PM 7:30 PM - 10:30 PM 2:30 AM - 5:30 AM	9:30 AM - 12:30 PM 4:30 PM - 7:30 PM 11:30 PM - 2:30 AM	6:30 AM - 9:30 AM 1:30 PM - 4:30 PM 8:30 PM - 11:30 PM
5:00 AM **to** **5:29 AM**	6:00 AM - 9:00 AM 1:00 PM - 4:00 PM 8:00 PM - 11:00 PM 3:00 AM - 6:00 AM	10:00 AM - 1:00 PM 5:00 PM - 8:00 PM 12:00 AM - 3:00 AM	7:00 AM -10:00 AM 2:00 PM - 5:00 PM 9:00 PM - 12:00 AM
5:30 AM **to** **5:59 AM**	6:30 AM - 9:30 AM 1:30 PM - 4:30 PM 8:30 PM - 11:30 PM 3:30 AM - 6:30 AM	10:30 AM - 1:30 PM 5:30 PM - 8:30 PM 12:30 AM - 3:30 AM	7:30 AM -10:30 AM 2:30 PM - 5:30 PM 9:30 PM - 12:30 AM

Refer to *Sample Chart* on page *36* for instructions.

LUCK CHART

WEDNESDAY	THURSDAY	FRIDAY	SATURDAY
2:00 AM - 5:00 AM 9:00 AM - 12:00 PM 4:00 PM - 7:00 PM 11:00 PM - 2:00 AM	6:00 AM - 9:00 AM 1:00 PM - 4:00 PM 8:00 PM - 11:00 PM	3:00 AM - 6:00 AM 10:00 AM - 1:00 PM 5:00 PM - 8:00 PM 12:00 AM - 3:00 AM	7:00 AM - 10:00 AM 2:00 PM - 5:00 PM 9:00 PM -12:00 AM
2:30 AM - 5:30 AM 9:30 AM - 12:30 PM 4:30 PM - 7:30 PM 11:30 PM - 2:30 AM	6:30 AM - 9:30 AM 1:30 PM - 4:30 PM 8:30 PM - 11:30 PM	3:30 AM - 6:30 AM 10:30 AM - 1:30 PM 5:30 PM - 8:30 PM 12:30 AM - 3:30 AM	7:30 AM - 10:30 AM 2:30 PM - 5:30 PM 9:30 PM - 12:30 AM
3:30 AM - 6:00 AM 10:00 AM - 1:00 PM 5:00 PM - 8:00 PM 12:00 AM - 3:00 AM	7:00 AM - 10:00 AM 2:00 PM - 5:00 PM 9:00 PM - 12:00 AM	4:00 AM - 7:00 AM 11:00 AM - 2:00 PM 6:00 PM - 9:00 PM 1:00 AM - 4:00 AM	8:00 AM - 11:00 AM 3:00 PM - 6:00 PM 10:00 PM - 1:00 AM
3:30 AM - 6:30 AM 10:30 AM - 1:30 PM 5:30 PM - 8:30 PM 12:30 AM - 3:30 AM	7:30 AM - 10:30 AM 2:30 PM - 5:30 PM 9:30 PM - 12:30 AM	4:30 AM - 7:30 AM 11:30 AM - 2:30 PM 6:30 PM - 9:30 PM 1:30 AM - 4:30 AM	8:30 AM -11:30 AM 3:30 PM - 6:30 PM 10:30 PM - 1:30 AM
4:00 AM - 7:00 AM 11:00 AM - 2:00 PM 6:00 PM - 9:00 PM 1:00 AM - 4:00 AM	8:00 AM - 11:00 AM 3:00 PM - 6:00 PM 10:00 PM - 1:00 AM	5:00 AM - 8:00 AM 12:00 PM - 3:00 PM 7:00 PM - 10:00 PM 2:00 AM - 5:00 AM	9:00 AM -12:00 PM 4:00 PM - 7:00 PM 11:00 PM - 2:00 AM
4:30 AM - 7:30 AM 11:30 AM - 2:30 PM 6:30 PM - 9:30 PM 1:30 AM - 4:30 AM	8:30 AM - 11:30 AM 3:30 PM - 6:30 PM 10:30 PM - 1:30 AM	5:30 AM - 8:30 AM 12:30 PM - 3:30 PM 7:30 PM - 10:30 PM 2:30 AM - 5:30 AM	9:30 AM -12:30 PM 4:30 PM - 7:30 PM 11:30 PM - 2:30 AM

SUNRISE	SUNDAY	MONDAY	TUESDAY
6:00 AM **to** **6:29 AM**	7:00 AM - 10:00 AM 2:00 PM - 5:00 PM 9:00 PM - 12:00 AM 4:00 AM - 7:00 AM	11:00 AM - 2:00 PM 6:00 PM - 9:00 PM 1:00 AM - 4:00 AM	8:00 AM - 11:00 AM 3:00 PM - 6:00 PM 10:00 PM - 1:00 AM
6:30 AM **to** **6:59 AM**	7:30 AM - 10:30 AM 2:30 PM - 5:30 PM 9:30 PM - 12:30 AM 4:30 AM - 7:30 AM	11:30 AM - 2:30 PM 6:30 PM - 9:30 PM 1:30 AM - 4:30 AM	8:30 AM - 11:30 AM 3:30 PM - 6:30 PM 10:30 PM - 1:30 AM
7:00 AM **to** **7:29 AM**	8:00 AM - 11:00 AM 3:00 PM - 6:00 PM 10:00 PM - 1:00 AM	4:00 AM - 7:00 AM 12:00 PM - 3:00 PM 7:00 PM - 10:00 PM 2:00 AM - 5:00 AM	9:00 AM - 12:00 PM 4:00 PM - 7:00 PM 11:00 PM - 2:00 AM
7:30 AM **to** **7:59 AM**	8:30 AM - 11:30 AM 3:30 PM - 6:30 PM 10:30 PM - 1:30 AM	4:30 AM - 7:30 AM 12:30 PM - 3:30 PM 7:30 PM - 10:30 PM 2:30 AM - 5:30 AM	9:30 AM - 12:30 PM 4:30 PM - 7:30 PM 11:30 PM - 2:30 AM
8:00 AM **to** **8:29 AM**	9:00 AM - 12:00 PM 4:00 PM - 7:00 PM 11:00 PM - 2:00 AM	5:00 AM - 8:00 AM 1:00 PM - 4:00 PM 8:00 PM - 11:00 PM 3:00 AM - 6:00 AM	10:00 AM -1:00 PM 5:00 PM - 8:00 PM 12:00 AM - 3:00 AM
8:30 AM **to** **8:59 AM**	9:30 AM - 12:30 PM 4:30 PM - 7:30 PM 11:30 PM - 2:30 AM	5:30 AM - 8:30 AM 1:30 PM - 4:30 PM 8:30 PM - 11:30 PM 3:30 AM - 6:30 AM	10:30 AM -1:30 PM 5:30 PM - 8:30 PM 12:30 AM - 3:30 AM

WEDNESDAY	THURSDAY	FRIDAY	SATURDAY
5:00 AM - 8:00 AM 12:00 AM - 3:00 PM 7:00 PM - 10:00 PM 2:00 AM - 5:00 AM	9:00 AM - 12:00 PM 4:00 PM -7:00 PM 11:00 PM - 2:00 AM	6:00 AM -9:00 AM 1:00 PM - 4:00 PM 8:00 PM -11:00 PM 3:00 AM - 6:00 AM	10:00 AM - 1:00 PM 5:00 PM - 8:00 PM 12:00 AM -3:00 AM
5:30 AM - 8:30 AM 12:30 PM - 3:30 PM 7:30 PM - 10:30 PM 2:30 AM - 5:30 AM	9:30 AM - 12:30 PM 4:30 PM - 7:30 PM 11:30 PM - 2:30 AM	6:30 AM - 9:30 AM 1:30 PM - 4:30 PM 8:30 PM - 11:30 PM 3:30 AM - 6:30 AM	10:30 AM - 1:30 PM 5:30 PM - 8:30 PM 12:30 AM - 3:30 AM
6:00 AM - 9:00 AM 1:00 PM - 4:00 PM 8:00 PM - 11:00 PM 3:00 AM - 6:00 AM	10:00 AM - 1:00 PM 5:00 PM - 8:00 PM 12:00 AM - 3:00 AM	7:00 AM - 10:00 AM 2:00 PM - 5:00 PM 9:00 PM - 12:00 AM 4:00 AM - 7:00 AM	11:00 AM - 2:00 PM 6:00 PM - 9:00 PM 1:00 AM - 4:00 AM
6:30 AM - 9:30 AM 1:30 PM - 4:30 PM 8:30 PM - 11:30 PM 3:30 AM - 6:30 AM	10:30 AM - 1:30 PM 5:30 PM - 8:30 PM 12:30 AM - 3:30 AM	7:30 AM - 10:30 AM 2:30 PM - 5:30 PM 9:30 PM - 12:30 AM 4:30 AM - 7:30 AM	11:30 AM - 2:30 PM 6:30 PM - 9:30 PM 1:30 AM - 4:30 AM
7:00 AM - 10:00 AM 2:00 PM - 5:00 PM 9:00 PM - 12:00 AM 4:00 AM - 7:00 AM	11:00 AM - 2:00 PM 6:00 PM - 9:00 PM 1:00 AM - 4:00 AM	8:00 AM - 11:00 AM 3:00 PM - 6:00 PM 10:00 PM - 1:00 AM 5:00 AM - 8:00 AM	12:00 PM -3:00 PM 7:00 PM - 10:00 PM 2:00 AM - 5:00 AM
7:30 AM - 10:30 AM 2:30 AM - 5:30 PM 9:30 PM - 12:30 AM 4:30 AM - 7:30 AM	11:30 AM - 2:30 PM 6:30 PM - 9:30 PM 1:30 AM - 4:30 AM	8:30 AM - 11:30 AM 3:30 PM - 6:30 PM 10:30 PM - 1:30 AM 5:30 AM - 8:30 AM	12:30 PM -3:30 PM 7:30 PM - 10:30 PM 2:30 AM - 5:30 AM

LIBRA

There is no getting away from the fact, that there are only nine numbers by which all our calculations on this earth are made. Beyond these nine numbers, all the rest are repetition, as 10 is a 1 with a 0 added, eleven (11) is 1+1=2; and so on. Every number, no matter how high, can be reduced to a single figure. That is why your lucky numbers first appear as single numbers, followed by numbers adding up to this single number, up to 31. However, any number over 31 which adds up to any of your single numbers, is also lucky for you.

Your first lucky number is - 9 - and all numbers adding up to 9, such as 18 and 27 - Lucky day Tuesday. This number was determined by combining your celestial number with other factors of your sun sign.

Your luckiest number is 9. Bear this in mind at all times. When you buy a ticket of any sort, make sure that the serial number has the predominant number 9 in it, and buy it during one of your lucky periods. Also a street address containing one or more 9's; horse number 9, player number 9 in a game; a 9 rolled in dice; room number 9 in a hotel/motel; and so on. These

are all considered fortunate for you. You can also combine number 9 with your other lucky numbers.

Your second lucky number is your birth date.

Your third lucky number is - 6 - as well as 15 and 24 - Lucky day Friday. This is the number assigned to the planet Venus, ruler of Libra.

NOTE: Since numbers 9 and 6 are part of the 3-6-9 combination, you will have a certain degree of luck with 3-12-21-30 (lucky day Thursday). All these numbers are especially lucky on Tuesday, Thursday and Friday.

BIRTH DATES

NUMBERS: 1 - 10 - 19 - 28
LUCKY DAYS: Sunday and Monday

People born on one of these dates are fortunate, because these numbers are related to 4-13-22-31 (lucky day Sunday), and the series of 1 and 4 are interrelated to 2-11-20-29 and 7-16-25 (lucky day Monday). Therefore, all these numbers are especially lucky on Sunday and Monday.

Your lucky yearly periods are; July 20th to August 28th and March 21st to April 28th.

NUMBERS: 2 - 11 - 20 - 29
LUCKY DAYS: Monday and Sunday

People born on one of these dates are fortunate, because these numbers are related to 7-16-25 (lucky day Monday), and the series of 2 and 7 are interrelated to numbers 1-10-19-28 and 4-13-22-31 (lucky day Sunday). Therefore, all these numbers are especially lucky on Monday and Sunday.

Your lucky yearly period is from June 21st to July 27th.

NUMBERS: 3 - 12 - 21 - 30
LUCKY DAY: Thursday

NOTE: Since these numbers are part of the 3-6-9 combination, you will have a certain degree of luck with 6-15-24 (lucky day Friday) and 9-18-27 (lucky day Tuesday). All these

numbers are especially lucky on Thursday, Tuesday and Friday.
Your lucky yearly periods are; February 19th to March 27th
and November 21st to December 27th

NUMBERS: 4 - 13 - 22 - 31
LUCKY DAYS: Sunday and Monday.
People born on one of these dates are fortunate, because
these numbers are related to 1-10-19-28 (lucky day Sunday), and
the series of 4 and 1 are interrelated to 2-11-20-29 and 7-16-25
(lucky day Monday). Therefore, all these numbers are especially
lucky on Sunday and Monday.
Your lucky yearly period is from June 21st to August 30th.

NUMBERS: 5 - 14 - 23
LUCKY DAY: Wednesday
You will also have a certain degree of luck on Fridays.
Your lucky yearly periods are; May 21st to June 27th and
August 21st to September 27th.

NUMBERS: 6 - 15 - 24
LUCKY DAY: Friday
If one of these dates is your birth date, these numbers are
extremely lucky for you, since they happen to be the same as your
third lucky number.
NOTE: Since these numbers are part of the 3-6-9
combination, you will have a certain degree of luck with
3-12-21-30 (lucky day Thursday) and 9-18-27 (lucky day
Tuesday). All these numbers are especially lucky on Friday,
Tuesday and Thursday.
Your lucky yearly periods are; April 20th to May 27th and
September 21st to October 27th.

NUMBERS: 7 - 16 - 25
LUCKY DAYS: Monday and Sunday.
People born on one of these dates are fortunate, because
these numbers are related to 2-11-20-29 (lucky day Monday), and
the series of 7 and 2 are interrelated to 1-10-19-28 and

4-13-22-31 (lucky day Sunday). Therefore, all these numbers are especially lucky on Monday and Sunday.

Your lucky yearly period is from June 21st to July 27th, and less strongly from this date to the end of August.

NUMBERS: 8 - 17 - 26
LUCKY DAY: Saturday

Since number 8 has a connection to number 4, you could have a certain degree of luck on Sundays.

Your lucky yearly periods are; from December 21st to December 31st, all of January up to February 26th.

NUMBERS: 9 - 18 - 27
LUCKY DAY: Tuesday

If one of these dates is your birth date, these numbers are extremely lucky for you since they happen to be the same as your first lucky number.

NOTE: Since these numbers are part of the 3-6-9 combination, you will have a certain degree of luck with 3-12-21-30 (lucky day Thursday) and 6-15-24 (lucky day Friday). All these numbers are especially lucky on Tuesday, Thursday and Friday.

Your lucky yearly periods are; March 21st to April 27th and October 21st to November 27th.

DECANS

Note: Decans are Stars or Constellations that rise once every ten days and by which the ancient Egyptians used to tell time.

There are certain periods during the year that are most fortunate for you, when your chances of winning are amplified even more.

If you were born on September 24, 25, 26, 27, 28, 29, 30 and October 1, 2 and 3 - the following periods are lucky for you.
January 21st to 30th
May 22nd to June 1st

July 24th to August 3rd
November 23rd to December 3rd

If you were born on October 4, 5, 6, 7, 8, 9, 10, 11, 12, 13
- the following periods are lucky for you.
January 31st to February 9th
June 1st to 12th
August 3rd to 14th
December 2nd to 12th

If you were born on October 14, 15, 16, 17, 18, 19, 20, 21,
22, 23 - the following periods are lucky for you.
February 9th to 19th
June 11th to 21st
August 12th to 23rd
December 11th to 22nd

The lucky periods in your Personal Luck Chart, and your lucky numbers, remain the same for the rest of your life. They are based on your birth date and the time of sunrise, which varies greatly throughout the year. I have provided you with sunrise times from 3:00 a.m. to 9:00 a.m.. Your lucky hours have been indicated for each hour of sunrise, for each day of the week. The only thing that changes is the time of sunrise, so all you have to do is check the sunrise time on any given day of the year, and go by the lucky hours listed for that time and day. For this reason, it doesn't matter if it's standard or daylight savings time. It also doesn't matter if you are at home or in another part of the world. Just go by the sunrise time for the location you are in, to determine your lucky hours.

Refer to *Sample Chart* on page *36* for instructions.

LIBRA PERSONAL

SUNRISE	SUNDAY	MONDAY	TUESDAY
3:00 AM to **3:29 AM**	3:00 AM - 6:00 AM 10:00 AM - 1:00 PM 5:00 PM - 8:00 PM 12:00 AM - 3:00 AM	7:00 AM - 10:00 AM 2:00 PM - 5:00 PM 9:00 PM - 12:00 AM	4:00 AM -7:00 AM 11:00 AM - 2:00 PM 6:00 PM - 9:00 PM
3:30 AM to **3:59 AM**	3:30 AM - 6:30 AM 10:30 AM - 1:30 PM 5:30 PM - 8:30 PM 12:30 AM - 3:30 AM	7:30 AM - 10:30 AM 2:30 PM - 5:30 PM 9:30 PM - 12:30 AM	4:30 AM -7:30 AM 11:30 AM - 2:30 PM 6:30 PM - 9:30 PM
4:00 AM to **4:29 AM**	4:00 AM -7:00 AM 11:00 AM - 2:00 PM 6:00 PM - 9:00 PM 1:00 AM - 4:00 AM	8:00 AM - 11:00 AM 3:00 PM - 6:00 PM 10:00 PM - 1:00 AM	5:00 AM - 8:00 AM 12:00 PM - 3:00 PM 7:00 PM - 10:00 PM
4:30 AM to **4:59 AM**	4:30 AM -7:30 AM 11:30 AM - 2:30 PM 6:30 PM - 9:30 PM 1:30 AM - 4:30 AM	8:30 AM - 11:30 AM 3:30 PM - 6:30 PM 10:30 PM - 1:30 AM	5:30 AM - 8:30 AM 12:30 PM - 3:30 PM 7:30 PM - 10:30 PM
5:00 AM to **5:29 AM**	5:00 AM - 8:00 AM 12:00 PM - 3:00 PM 7:00 PM - 10:00 PM 2:00 AM - 5:00 AM	9:00 AM - 12:00 PM 4:00 PM - 7:00 PM 11:00 PM - 2:00 AM	6:00 AM - 9:00 AM 1:00 PM - 4:00 PM 8:00 PM - 11:00 PM
5:30 AM to **5:59 AM**	5:30 AM - 8:30 AM 12:30 PM - 3:30 PM 7:30 PM - 10:30 PM 2:30 AM - 5:30 AM	9:30 AM - 12:30 PM 4:30 PM -7:30 PM 11:30 PM - 2:30 AM	6:30 AM - 9:30 AM 1:30 PM - 4:30 PM 8:30 PM - 11:30 PM

Refer to *Sample Chart* on page *36* for instructions.

LUCK CHART

WEDNESDAY	THURSDAY	FRIDAY	SATURDAY
8:00 AM - 11:00 AM 3:00 PM - 6:00 PM 10:00 PM - 1:00 AM	5:00 AM - 8:00 AM 12:00 PM - 3:00 PM 7:00 PM - 10:00 PM	2:00 AM - 5:00 AM 9:00 AM - 12:00 AM 4:00 PM - 7:00 PM 11:00 PM - 2:00 AM	6:00 AM - 9:00 AM 1:00 PM - 4:00 PM 8:00 PM - 11:00 PM
8:30 AM - 11:30 AM 3:30 PM - 6:30 PM 10:30 PM - 1:30 AM	5:30 AM - 8:30 AM 12:30 PM - 3:30 PM 7:30 PM - 10:30 PM	2:30 AM - 5:30 AM 9:30 AM - 12:30 PM 4:30 PM - 7:30 PM 11:30 PM - 2:30 AM	6:30 AM -9:30 AM 1:30 PM - 4:30 PM 8:30 PM - 11:30 PM •
9:00 AM - 12:00 PM 4:00 PM - 7:00 PM 11:00 PM - 2:00 AM	6:00 AM - 9:00 AM 1:00 PM - 4:00 PM 8:00 PM - 11:00 PM	3:00 AM - 6:00 AM 10:00 AM - 1:00 PM 5:00 PM - 8:00 PM 12:00 PM - 3:00 AM	7:00 AM - 10:00 AM 2:00 PM - 5:00 PM 9:00 PM - 12:00 AM
9:30 AM - 12:30 PM 4:30 PM - 7:30 PM 11:30 PM - 2:30 PM	6:30 AM -9:30 AM 1:30 PM - 4:30 PM 8:30 PM - 11:30 PM	3:30 AM - 6:30 AM 10:30 AM - 1:30 PM 5:30 PM - 8:30 PM 12:30 AM - 3:30 AM	7:30 AM - 10:30 AM 2:30 PM - 5:30 PM 9:30 PM - 12:30 AM
10:00 AM - 1:00 PM 5:00 PM - 8:00 PM 12:00 PM - 3:00 AM	7:00 AM - 10:00 AM 2:00 PM - 5:00 PM 9:00 PM - 12:00 AM	4:00 AM - 7:00 AM 11:00 AM - 2:00 PM 6:00 PM - 9:00 PM 1:00 AM - 4:00 AM	8:00 AM - 11:00 AM 3:00 PM - 6:00 PM 10:00 PM - 1:00 AM
10:30 AM - 1:30 PM 5:30 PM - 8:30 PM 12:30 AM - 3:30 AM	7:30 AM - 10:30 AM 2:30 PM - 5:30 PM 9:30 PM - 12:30 AM	4:30 AM - 7:30 AM 11:30 AM - 2:30 PM 6:30 PM -9:30 PM 1:30 AM - 4:30 AM	8:30 AM - 11:30 AM 3:30 PM - 6:30 PM 10:30 PM - 1:30 AM

SUNRISE	SUNDAY	MONDAY	TUESDAY
6:00 AM to **6:29 AM**	6:00 AM - 9:00 AM 1:00 PM - 4:00 PM 8:00 PM - 11:00 PM 3:00 AM - 6:00 AM	10:00 AM - 1:00 PM 5:00 PM - 8:00 PM 12:00 AM - 3:00 AM	7:00 AM - 10:00 AM 2:00 PM - 5:00 PM 9:00 PM - 12:00 AM
6:30 AM to **6:59 AM**	6:30 AM - 9:30 AM 1:30 PM - 4:30 PM 8:30 PM - 11:30 PM 3:30 AM - 6:30 AM	10:30 AM - 1:30 PM 5:30 PM - 8:30 PM 12:30 AM - 3:30 AM	7:30 AM - 10:30 AM 2:30 PM - 5:30 PM 9:30 PM - 12:30 AM
7:00 AM to **7:29 AM**	7:00 AM - 10:00 AM 2:00 PM - 5:00 PM 9:00 PM - 12:00 AM	4:00 AM - 7:00 AM 11:00 AM - 2:00 PM 6:00 PM - 9:00 PM 1:00 AM - 4:00 AM	8:00 AM - 11:00 AM 3:00 PM - 6:00 PM 10:00 PM - 1:00 AM
7:30 AM to **7:59 AM**	7:30 AM - 10:30 AM 2:30 PM - 5:30 PM 9:30 PM - 12:30 AM	4:30 AM - 7:30 AM 11:30 AM - 2:30 PM 6:30 PM - 9:30 PM 1:30 AM - 4:30 AM	8:30 AM - 11:30 AM 3:30 PM - 6:30 PM 10:30 PM - 1:30 AM
8:00 AM to **8:29 AM**	8:00 AM - 11:00 AM 3:00 PM - 6:00 PM 10:00 PM - 1:00 AM	5:00 AM - 8:00 AM 12:00 PM - 3:00 PM 7:00 PM - 10:00 PM 2:00 AM - 5:00 AM	9:00 AM - 12:00 PM 4:00 PM - 7:00 PM 11:00 PM - 2:00 AM
8:30 AM to **8:59 AM**	8:30 AM - 11:30 AM 3:30 PM - 6:30 PM 10:30 PM - 1:30 AM	5:30 AM - 8:30 AM 12:30 PM - 3:30 PM 7:30 PM - 10:30 PM 2:30 AM - 5:30 AM	9:30 AM - 12:30 PM 4:30 PM - 7:30 PM 11:30 PM - 2:30 AM

WEDNESDAY	THURSDAY	FRIDAY	SATURDAY
11:00 AM - 2:00 PM 6:00 PM - 9:00 PM 1:00 AM - 4:00 AM	8:00 AM - 11:00 AM 3:00 PM - 6:00 PM 10:00 PM - 1:00 AM	5:00 AM - 8:00 AM 12:00 PM - 3:00 PM 7:00 PM - 10:00 AM 2:00 AM - 5:00 AM	9:00 AM - 12:00 PM 4:00 PM - 7:00 PM 11:00 PM - 2:00 AM
11:30 AM - 2:30 PM 6:30 PM - 9:30 PM 1:30 AM - 4:30 AM	8:30 AM - 11:30 AM 3:30 PM - 6:30 PM 10:30 PM - 1:30 AM	5:30 AM - 8:30 AM 12:30 PM - 3:30 PM 7:30 PM - 10:30 AM 2:30 AM - 5:30 AM	9:30 AM - 12:30 PM 4:30 PM - 7:30 PM 11:30 PM - 2:30 AM
12:00 PM - 3:00 PM 7:00 PM - 10:00 PM 2:00 AM - 5:00 AM	9:00 AM - 12:00 PM 4:00 PM - 7:00 PM 11:00 PM - 2:00 AM	6:00 AM - 9:00 AM 1:00 PM - 4:00 PM 8:00 PM -11:00 AM 3:00 AM - 6:00 AM	10:00 AM - 1:00 PM 5:00 PM - 8:00 PM 12:00 AM - 3:00 AM
12:30 PM - 3:30 PM 7:30 PM - 10:30 PM 2:30 AM - 5:30 AM	9:30 AM - 12:30 PM 4:30 PM - 7:30 PM 11:30 PM - 2:30 AM	6:30 AM - 9:30 AM 1:30 PM - 4:30 PM 8:30 PM - 11:30 AM 3:30 AM - 6:30 AM	10:30 AM - 1:30 PM 5:30 PM - 8:30 PM 12:30 AM - 3:30 AM
1:00 PM - 4:00 PM 8:00 PM -11:00 AM 3:00 AM - 6:00 AM	10:00 AM - 1:00 PM 5:00 PM - 8:00 PM 12:00 AM - 3:00 AM	7:00 AM - 10:00 AM 2:00 PM - 5:00 PM 9:00 PM - 12:00 PM 4:00 AM - 7:00 AM	11:00 AM - 2:00 PM 6:00 PM - 9:00 PM 1:00 AM - 4:00 AM
1:30 PM - 4:30 PM 8:30 PM - 11:30 PM 3:30 AM - 6:30 AM	10:30 AM - 1:30 PM 5:30 PM - 8:30 PM 12:30 AM - 3:30 AM	7:30 AM - 10:30 AM 2:30 PM - 5:30 PM 9:30 PM - 12:30 PM 4:30 AM - 7:30 AM	11:30 AM - 2:30 PM 6:30 PM - 9:30 PM 1:30 AM - 4:30 AM

SCORPIO

There is no getting away from the fact, that there are only nine numbers by which all our calculations on earth are made. Beyond these nine numbers, all the rest are repetition, as 10 is a 1 with a 0 added, eleven (11) is 1+1=2; and so on. Every number, no matter how high, can be reduced to a single figure. This is why your lucky numbers first appear as single numbers, followed by numbers adding up to this single number, up to 31. However, any number over 31 which adds up to any of your single lucky numbers, is also lucky for you.

Your first lucky number is - 8 - and all numbers adding up to 8, such as 17 and 26 - Lucky day Saturday. This number was determined by combining your celestial number with other factors of your sun sign.

Your luckiest number is 8. Bear this in mind at all times. When you buy a ticket of any sort, make sure that the serial number has the predominant number 8 in it, and buy it during one of your lucky periods. Also a street address containing one or more 8's; horse number 8, player number 8 in a game; an 8 rolled in dice; room number 8 in a hotel/motel; and so on. These

are all considered fortunate for you. You can also combine number 8 with your other lucky numbers.

Your second lucky number is your birth date.

Your third lucky number is - 9 - as well as 18 and 27 - Lucky day Tuesday. This is the number assigned to the planet Mars, ruler of Scorpio.

NOTE: Since number 9 is part of the 3-6-9 combination, you will have a certain degree of luck with 3-12-21-30 (lucky day Thursday) and 6-15-24 (lucky day Friday). All these numbers are especially lucky on Tuesday, Thursday and Friday.

BIRTH DATES

NUMBERS: 1 - 10 - 19 - 28
LUCKY DAYS: Sunday and Monday

People born on one of these dates are fortunate, because these numbers are related to 4-13-22-31 (lucky day Sunday), and the series of 1 and 4 are interrelated to 2-11-20-29 and 7-16-25 (lucky day Monday). Therefore, all these numbers are especially lucky on Sunday and Monday.

Your lucky yearly periods are; July 20th to August 28th and March 21st to April 28th.

NUMBERS: 2 - 11 - 20 - 29
LUCKY DAYS: Monday and Sunday

People born on one of these dates are fortunate, because these numbers are related to 7-16-25 (lucky day Monday), and the series of 2 and 7 are interrelated to 1-10-19-28 and 4-13-22-31 (lucky day Sunday). Therefore, all these numbers are especially lucky on Monday and Sunday.

Your lucky yearly period is from June 21st to July 27th.

NUMBERS: 3 - 12 - 21 - 30
LUCKY DAY: Thursday

NOTE: Since these numbers are part of the 3-6-9 combination, you will have a certain degree of luck with 6-15-24 (lucky day Friday) and 9-18-27 (lucky day Tuesday). All these

numbers are especially lucky on Thursday, Tuesday and Friday.

Your lucky yearly periods are; February 19th to March 27th and November 21st to December 27th.

NUMBERS: 4 - 13 - 22 - 31
LUCKY DAYS: Sunday and Monday.

People born on one of these dates are fortunate, because these numbers are related to 1-10-19-28 (lucky day Sunday), and the series of 4 and 1 are interrelated to 2-11-20-29 and 7-16-25 (lucky day Monday). Therefore, all these numbers are especially lucky on Sunday and Monday.

Your lucky yearly period is from June 21st to August 30th.

NUMBERS: 5 - 14 - 23
LUCKY DAY: Wednesday

You will also have a certain degree of luck on Fridays.

Your lucky yearly periods are; May 21st to June 27th and August 21st to September 27th.

NUMBERS: 6 - 15 - 24
LUCKY DAY: Friday

NOTE: Since these numbers are part of the 3-6-9 combination, you will have a certain degree of luck with 3-12-21-30 (lucky day Thursday) and 9-18-27 (lucky day Tuesday). All these numbers are especially lucky on Friday, Tuesday and Thursday.

Your lucky yearly periods are; April 20th to May 27th and September 21st to October 27th.

NUMBERS: 7 - 16 - 25
LUCKY DAYS: Monday and Sunday.

People born on one of these dates are fortunate, because these numbers are related to 2-11-20-29 (lucky day Monday), and the series of 7 and 2 are interrelated to 1-10-19-28 and 4-13-22-31 (lucky day Sunday). Therefore, all these numbers are especially lucky on Monday and Sunday.

Your lucky yearly period is from June 21st to July 27th, and less strongly from this date to the end of August.

NUMBERS: 8 - 17 - 26
LUCKY DAY: Saturday

If one of these dates is your birth date, these numbers are extremely fortunate for you, since they happen to be the same as your first lucky number. Since number 8 has a connection to number 4, you could have a certain degree of luck on Sundays.

Your lucky yearly periods are; from December 21st to December 31st, all of January up to February 26th.

NUMBERS: 9 - 18 - 27
LUCKY DAY: Tuesday

If one of these dates is your birth date, these numbers are extremely lucky for you since they happen to be the same as your third lucky number.

NOTE: Since these numbers are part of the 3-6-9 combination, you will have a certain degree of luck with 3-12-21-30 (lucky day Thursday) and 6-15-24 (lucky day Friday). All these numbers are especially lucky on Tuesday, Thursday and Friday.

Your lucky yearly periods are; March 21st to April 27th and October 21st to November 27th.

DECANS

Note: Decans are Stars or Constellations that rise once every ten days and by which the ancient Egyptians used to tell time.

There are certain periods during the year that are most fortunate for you, when your chances of winning are amplified even more.

If you were born on October 24, 25, 26, 27, 28, 29, 30, 31 and November 1 and 2 - the following periods are lucky for you.

> February 20th to 29th
> June 22nd to July 2nd
> August 24th to September 3rd
> December 21st to 31st

If you were born on November 3, 4, 5, 6, 7, 8, 9, 10, 11, 12 - the following periods are lucky for you.

January 1st to 11th
March 1st to 10th
July 2nd to 13th
September 3rd to 14th

If you were born on November 13, 14, 15, 16, 17, 18, 19, 20, 21, 22 - the following periods are lucky for you.

January 11th to 20th
March 10th to 20th
July 12th to 23rd
September 13th to 23rd

The lucky periods in your Personal Luck Chart, and your lucky numbers, remain the same for the rest of your life. They are based on your birth date and the time of sunrise, which varies greatly throughout the year. I have provided you with sunrise times from 3:00 a.m. to 9:00 a.m.. Your lucky hours have been indicated for each hour of sunrise, for each day of the week. The only thing that changes is the time of sunrise, so all you have to do is check the sunrise time on any given day of the year, and go by the lucky hours listed for that time and day. For this reason, it doesn't matter if it's standard or daylight savings time. It also doesn't matter if you are at home or in another part of the world. Just go by the sunrise time for the location you are in, to determine your lucky hours.

Refer to **Sample Chart** on page *36* for instructions.

SCORPIO PERSONAL

SUNRISE	SUNDAY	MONDAY	TUESDAY
3:00 AM to **3:29 AM**	8:00 AM - 11:00 AM 3:00 PM - 6:00 PM 10:00 PM - 1:00 AM	5:00 AM - 8:00 AM 12:00 PM - 3:00 PM 7:00 PM - 10:00 PM	2:00 AM - 5:00 AM 9:00 AM - 12:00 PM 4:00 PM - 7:00 PM 11:00 PM - 2:00 AM
3:30 AM to **3:59 AM**	8:30 AM - 11:30 AM 3:30 PM - 6:30 PM 10:30 PM - 1:30 AM	5:30 AM - 8:30 AM 12:30 PM - 3:30 PM 7:30 PM - 10:30 PM	2:30 AM - 5:30 AM 9:30 AM - 12:30 PM 4:30 PM - 7:30 PM 11:30 PM - 2:30 AM
4:00 AM to **4:29 AM**	9:00 AM - 12:00 PM 4:00 PM - 7:00 PM 11:00 PM - 2:00 AM	6:00 AM - 9:00 AM 1:00 PM - 4:00 PM 8:00 PM - 11:00 PM	3:00 AM - 6:00 AM 10:00 AM - 1:00 PM 5:00 PM - 8:00 PM 12:00 AM - 3:00 AM
4:30 AM to **4:59 AM**	9:30 AM - 12:30 PM 4:30 PM - 7:30 PM 11:30 PM - 2:30 AM	6:30 AM - 9:30 AM 1:30 PM - 4:30 PM 8:30 PM - 11:30 PM	3:30 AM - 6:30 AM 10:30 AM - 1:30 PM 5:30 PM - 8:30 PM 12:30 AM - 3:30 AM
5:00 AM to **5:29 AM**	10:00 AM - 1:00 PM 5:00 PM - 8:00 PM 12:00 AM - 3:00 AM	7:00 AM - 10:00 AM 2:00 PM - 5:00 PM 9:00 PM - 12:00 AM	4:00 AM -7:00 AM 11:00 AM - 2:00 PM 6:00 PM - 9:00 PM 1:00 AM - 4:00 AM
5:30 AM to **5:59 AM**	10:30 AM - 1:30 PM 5:30 PM - 8:30 PM 12:30 AM - 3:30 AM	7:30 AM - 10:30 AM 2:30 PM - 5:30 PM 9:30 PM - 12:30 AM	4:30 AM -7:30 AM 11:30 AM - 2:30 PM 6:30 PM - 9:30 PM 1:30 AM - 4:30 AM

Refer to *Sample Chart* on page *36* for instructions.

LUCK CHART

WEDNESDAY	THURSDAY	FRIDAY	SATURDAY
6:00 AM - 9:00 AM 1:00 PM - 4:00 PM 8:00 PM - 11:00 PM	3:00 AM - 6:00 AM 10:00 AM - 1:00 PM 5:00 PM - 8:00 PM 12:00 AM - 3:00 AM	7:00 AM - 10:00 AM 2:00 PM - 5:00 PM 9:00 PM - 12:00 AM	4:00 AM - 7:00 AM 11:00 AM - 2:00 PM 6:00 PM - 9:00 PM 1:00 AM - 4:00 AM
6:30 AM - 9:30 AM 1:30 PM - 4:30 PM 8:30 PM - 11:30 PM	3:30 AM - 6:30 AM 10:30 AM - 1:30 PM 5:30 PM - 8:30 PM 12:30 AM - 3:30 AM	7:30 AM - 10:30 AM 2:30 PM - 5:30 PM 9:30 PM - 12:30 AM	4:30 AM - 7:30 AM 11:30 AM - 2:30 PM 6:30 PM - 9:30 PM 1:30 AM - 4:30 AM
7:00 AM - 10:00 AM 2:00 PM - 5:00 PM 9:00 PM - 12:00 AM	4:00 AM - 7:00 AM 11:00 AM - 2:00 PM 6:00 PM - 9:00 PM 1:00 AM - 4:00 AM	8:00 AM - 11:00 AM 3:00 PM - 6:00 PM 10:00 PM - 1:00 AM	5:00 AM - 8:00 AM 12:00 PM - 3:00 PM 7:00 PM - 10:00 PM 2:00 AM - 5:00 AM
7:30 AM - 10:30 AM 2:30 PM - 5:30 PM 9:30 PM - 12:30 AM	4:30 AM - 7:30 AM 11:30 AM - 2:30 PM 6:30 PM - 9:30 PM 1:30 AM - 4:30 AM	8:30 AM - 11:30 AM 3:30 PM - 6:30 PM 10:30 PM - 1:30 AM	5:30 AM - 8:30 AM 12:30 PM - 3:30 PM 7:30 PM - 10:30 PM 2:30 AM - 5:30 AM
8:00 AM - 11:00 AM 3:00 PM - 6:00 PM 10:00 PM - 1:00 AM	5:00 AM - 8:00 AM 12:00 PM - 3:00 PM 7:00 PM - 10:00 PM 2:00 AM - 5:00 AM	9:00 AM - 12:00 PM 4:00 PM - 7:00 PM 11:00 PM - 2:00 AM	6:00 AM - 9:00 AM 1:00 PM - 4:00 PM 8:00 PM - 11:00 PM 3:00 AM - 6:00 AM
8:30 AM - 11:30 AM 3:30 PM - 6:30 PM 10:30 PM - 1:30 AM	5:30 AM - 8:30 AM 12:30 PM - 3:30 PM 7:30 PM - 10:30 PM 2:30 AM - 5:30 AM	9:30 AM - 12:30 PM 4:30 PM - 7:30 PM 11:30 PM - 2:30 PM	6:30 AM -9:30 AM 1:30 PM - 4:30 PM 8:30 PM - 11:30 PM 3:30 AM - 6:30 AM

SUNRISE	SUNDAY	MONDAY	TUESDAY
6:00 AM to **6:29 AM**	11:00 AM - 2:00 PM 6:00 PM - 9:00 PM 1:00 AM - 4:00 AM	8:00 AM - 11:00 AM 3:00 PM - 6:00 PM 10:00 PM - 1:00 AM	5:00 AM - 8:00 AM 12:00 PM - 3:00 PM 7:00 PM - 10:00 PM 2:00 AM - 5:00 AM
6:30 AM to **6:59 AM**	11:30 AM - 2:30 PM 6:30 PM - 9:30 PM 1:30 AM - 4:30 AM	8:30 AM - 11:30 AM 3:30 PM - 6:30 PM 10:30 PM - 1:30 AM	5:30 AM - 8:30 AM 12:30 PM - 3:30 PM 7:30 PM - 10:30 PM 2:30 AM - 5:30 AM
7:00 AM to **7:29 AM**	12:00 PM -3:30 PM 7:00 PM - 10:00 PM 2:00 AM - 5:00 AM	9:00 AM - 12:00 PM 4:00 PM - 7:00 PM 11:00 PM - 2:00 AM	6:00 AM - 9:00 AM 1:00 PM - 4:00 PM 8:00 PM - 11:00 PM 3:00 AM - 6:00 AM
7:30 AM to **7:59 AM**	12:30 AM -3:30 PM 7:30 PM - 10:30 PM 2:30 AM - 5:30 AM	9:30 AM - 12:30 PM 4:30 PM - 7:30 PM 11:30 PM - 2:30 AM	6:30 AM - 9:30 AM 1:30 PM - 4:30 PM 8:30 PM - 11:30 PM 3:30 AM - 6:30 AM
8:00 AM to **8:29 AM**	1:00 PM - 4:00 PM 8:00 PM - 11:00 PM 3:00 AM - 6:00 AM	10:00 AM -1:00 PM 5:00 PM - 8:00 PM 12:00 AM - 3:00 AM	7:00 AM - 10:00 AM 2:00 PM - 5:00 PM 9:00 PM - 12:00 AM
8:30 AM to **8:59 AM**	1:30 PM - 4:30 PM 8:30 PM - 11:30 PM 3:30 AM - 6:30 AM	10:30 AM -1:30 PM 5:30 PM - 8:30 PM 12:30 AM - 3:30 AM	7:30 AM - 10:30 AM 2:30 PM - 5:30 PM 9:30 PM - 12:30 AM

WEDNESDAY	THURSDAY	FRIDAY	SATURDAY
9:00 AM - 12:00 PM 4:00 PM -7:00 PM 11:00 PM - 2:00 AM	6:00 AM -9:00 AM 1:00 PM - 4:00 PM 8:00 PM -11:00 PM 3:00 AM - 6:00 AM	10:00 AM - 1:00 PM 5:00 PM - 8:00 PM 12:00 AM -3:00 AM	7:00 AM - 10:00 AM 2:00 PM - 5:00 PM 9:00 PM - 12:00 AM 4:00 AM - 7:00 AM
9:30 AM - 12:30 PM 4:30 PM - 7:30 PM 11:30 PM - 2:30 AM	6:30 AM - 9:30 AM 1:30 PM - 4:30 PM 8:30 PM - 11:30 PM 3:30 AM - 6:30 AM	10:30 AM - 1:30 PM 5:30 PM - 8:30 PM 12:30 AM - 3:30 AM	7:30 AM - 10:30 AM 2:30 PM - 5:30 PM 9:30 PM - 12:30 AM 4:30 AM - 7:30 AM
10:00 AM - 1:00 PM 5:00 PM - 8:00 PM 12:00 AM - 3:00 AM	7:00 AM - 10:00 AM 2:00 PM - 5:00 PM 9:00 PM - 12:00 AM	4:00 AM - 7:00 AM 11:00 AM - 2:00 PM 6:00 PM - 9:00 PM 1:00 AM - 4:00 AM	8:00 AM - 11:00 AM 3:00 PM - 6:00 PM 10:00 PM - 1:00 AM 5:00 AM - 8:00 AM
10:30 AM - 1:30 PM 5:30 PM - 8:30 PM 12:30 AM - 3:30 AM	7:30 AM - 10:30 AM 2:30 PM - 5:30 PM 9:30 PM - 12:30 AM	4:30 AM - 7:30 AM 11:30 AM - 2:30 PM 6:30 PM - 9:30 PM 1:30 AM - 4:30 AM	8:30 AM - 11:30 AM 3:30 PM - 6:30 PM 10:30 PM - 1:30 AM 5:30 AM - 8:30 AM
4:00 AM - 7:00 AM 11:00 AM - 2:00 PM 6:00 PM - 9:00 PM 1:00 AM - 4:00 AM	8:00 AM - 11:00 AM 3:00 PM - 6:00 PM 10:00 PM - 1:00 AM	5:00 AM - 8:00 AM 12:00 AM - 3:00 PM 7:00 PM - 10:00 PM 2:00 AM - 5:00 AM	9:00 AM - 12:00 PM 4:00 PM - 7:00 PM 11:00 PM - 2:00 AM 6:00 AM - 9:00 AM
4:30 AM - 7:30 AM 11:30 AM - 2:30 PM 6:30 PM - 9:30 PM 1:30 AM - 4:30 AM	8:30 AM - 11:30 AM 3:30 PM - 6:30 PM 10:30 PM - 1:30 AM	5:30 AM - 8:30 AM 12:30 PM - 3:30 PM 7:30 PM - 10:30 PM 2:30 AM - 5:30 AM	9:30 AM - 12:30 PM 4:30 PM - 7:30 PM 11:30 PM - 2:30 AM 6:30 AM - 9:30 AM

SAGITTARIUS

There is no getting away from the fact, that there are only nine numbers by which all our calculations on this earth are made. Beyond these nine numbers, all the rest are repetition, as 10 is a 1 with a 0 added, eleven (11) is 1+1=2; and so on. Every number, no matter how high, can be reduced to a single figure. This is why your lucky numbers first appear as single numbers, followed by numbers adding up to this single number, up to 31. However, any number over 31 which adds up to any of your single lucky numbers, is also lucky for you.

Your first lucky number is - 8 - and all numbers adding up to 8, such as 17 and 26 - Lucky day Saturday. This number was determined by combining your celestial number with other factors of your sun sign.

Your luckiest number is 8. Bear this in mind at all times. When you buy a ticket of any sort, make sure that the serial number has the predominant number 8 in it, and buy it during one of your lucky periods. Also a street address containing one or more 8's; horse number 8, player number 8 in a game; an 8 rolled in dice; room number 8 in a hotel/motel; and so on. These

are all considered fortunate for you. You can also combine
number 8 with your other lucky numbers.

Your second lucky number is your birth date.

Your third lucky number is - 3 - as well as 12-21-30 -
Lucky day Thursday. This is the number assigned to the planet
Jupiter, ruler of Sagittarius.

NOTE: Since number 3 is part of the 3-6-9 combination,
you will have a certain degree of luck with 6-15-24 (lucky day
Friday) and 9-18-27 (lucky day Tuesday). All these numbers are
especially lucky on Tuesday, Thursday and Friday.

BIRTH DATES

NUMBERS: 1 - 10 - 19 - 28
LUCKY DAYS: Sunday and Monday

People born on one of these dates are fortunate, because
these numbers are related to 4-13-22-31 (lucky day Sunday), and
the series of 1 and 4 are interrelated to 2-11-20-29 and 7-16-25
(lucky day Monday). Therefore, all these numbers are especially
lucky on Sunday and Monday.

Your lucky yearly periods are; July 20th to August 28th and
March 21st to April 28th.

NUMBERS: 2 - 11 - 20 - 29
LUCKY DAYS: Monday and Sunday.

People born on one of these dates are fortunate, because
these numbers are related to 7-16-25 (lucky day Monday), and the
series of 2 and 7 are interrelated to 1-10-19-28 and 4-13-22-31
(lucky day Sunday). Therefore, all these numbers are especially
lucky on Monday and Sunday.

Your lucky yearly period is from June 21st to July 27th.

NUMBERS: 3 - 12 - 21 - 30
LUCKY DAY: Thursday

If one of these dates is your birth date, these numbers are
extremely lucky for you, since they happen to be the same as your

third lucky number.

NOTE: Since these numbers are part of the 3-6-9 combination, you will have a certain degree of luck with 6-15-24 (lucky day Friday) and 9-18-27 (lucky day Tuesday). All these numbers are especially lucky on Thursday, Tuesday and Friday.

Your lucky yearly periods are; February 19th to March 27th and November 21st to December 27th.

NUMBERS: 4 - 13 - 22 - 31
LUCKY DAYS: Sunday and Monday
    People born on one of these dates are fortunate, because these numbers are related to 1-10-19-28 (lucky day Sunday), and the series of 4 and 1 are interrelated to 2-11-20-29 and 7-16-25 (lucky day Monday). Therefore, all these numbers are especially lucky on Sunday and Monday.

Your lucky yearly period is from June 21st to August 30th.

NUMBERS: 5 - 14 - 23
LUCKY DAY: Wednesday
    You will also have a certain degree of luck on Fridays.
    Your lucky yearly periods are; May 21st to June 27th and August 21st to September 27th.

NUMBERS: 6 - 15 - 24
LUCKY DAY: Friday
    NOTE: Since these numbers are part of the 3-6-9 combination, you will have a certain degree of luck with 3-12-21-30 (lucky day Thursday) and 9-18-27 (lucky day Tuesday). All these numbers are especially lucky on Friday, Tuesday and Thursday.
    Your lucky yearly periods are; April 20th to May 27th and September 21st to October 27th.

NUMBERS: 7 - 16 - 25
LUCKY DAYS: Monday and Sunday.
    People born on one of these dates are fortunate, because these numbers are related to 2-11-20-29 (lucky day Monday), and

the series of 7 and 2 are interrelated to 1-10-19-28 and 4-13-22-31 (lucky day Sunday). Therefore, all these numbers are especially lucky on Monday and Sunday.

Your lucky yearly period is from June 21st to July 27th, and less strongly from this date to the end of August.

NUMBERS: 8 - 17 - 26
LUCKY DAY: Saturday

If one of these dates is your birth date, these numbers are extremely lucky for you, since they happen to be the same as your first lucky number.

Since number 8 has a connection to number 4, you could have a certain degree of luck on Sundays.

Your lucky yearly periods are; from December 21st to December 31st, all of January up to February 26th.

NUMBERS: 9 - 18 - 27
LUCKY DAY: Tuesday

NOTE: Since these numbers are part of the 3-6-9 combination, you will have a certain degree of luck with 3-12-21-30 (lucky day Thursday) and 6-15-24 (lucky day Friday). All these numbers are especially lucky on Tuesday, Thursday and Friday.

Your lucky yearly periods are; March 21st to April 27th and October 21st to November 27th.

DECANS

Note: Decans are Stars or Constellations that rise once every ten days and by which the ancient Egyptians used to tell time.

There are certain periods during the year that are most fortunate for you, when the chances of winning are amplified even more.

If you were born on November 23, 24, 25, 26, 27, 28, 29, 30 and December 1 & 2 - the following periods are lucky for you.
January 21st to 30th

March 21ˢᵗ to 31ˢᵗ
July 23ʳᵈ to August 3ʳᵈ
September 23ʳᵈ to October 4ᵗʰ

If you were born on December 3, 4, 5, 6, 7, 8, 9, 10, 11, 12 - the following periods are lucky for you.
January 31ˢᵗ to February 9ᵗʰ
April 1ˢᵗ to 11ᵗʰ
August 12ᵗʰ to 23rd
October 3ʳᵈ to 14ᵗʰ

If you were born on December 13, 14, 15, 16, 17, 18, 19, 20, 21, 22 - the following periods are lucky for you.
February 9ᵗʰ to 20ᵗʰ
April 10ᵗʰ to 20ᵗʰ
August 13ᵗʰ to 23ʳᵈ
October 12ᵗʰ to 23ʳᵈ

The lucky periods in your Personal Luck Chart, and your lucky numbers, remain the same for the rest of your life. They are based on your birth date and the time of sunrise, which varies greatly throughout the year. I have provided you with sunrise times from 3:00 a.m. to 9:00 a.m. Your lucky hours have been indicated for each hour of sunrise, for each day of the week. The only thing that changes is the time of sunrise, so all you have to do is check the sunrise time on any given day of the year, and go by the lucky hours listed for that time and day. For this reason, it doesn't matter if it's standard or daylight savings time. It also doesn't matter if you are at home or in another part of the world. Just go by the sunrise time for the location you are in, to determine your lucky hours.

Refer to *Sample Chart* on page *36* for instructions.

SAGITTARIUS

SUNRISE	SUNDAY	MONDAY	TUESDAY
3:00 AM **to** **3:29 AM**	7:00 AM -10:00 AM 2:00 PM - 5:00 PM 9:00 PM - 12:00 AM	4:00 AM - 7:00 AM 11:00 AM - 2:00 PM 6:00 PM - 9:00 PM 1:00 AM - 4:00 AM	8:00 AM - 11:00 AM 3:00 PM - 6:00 PM 10:00 PM - 1:00 AM
3:30 AM **to** **3:59 AM**	7:30 AM -10:30 AM 2:30 PM - 5:30 PM 9:30 PM - 12:30 AM	4:30 AM - 7:30 AM 11:30 AM - 2:30 PM 6:30 PM - 9:30 PM 1:30 AM - 4:30 AM	8:30 AM - 11:30 AM 3:30 PM - 6:30 PM 10:30 PM - 1:30 AM
4:00 AM **to** **4:29 AM**	8:00 AM -11:00 AM 3:00 PM - 6:00 PM 10:00 PM - 1:00 AM	5:00 AM - 8:00 AM 12:00 PM - 3:00 PM 7:00 PM - 10:00 PM 2:00 AM - 5:00 AM	9:00 AM - 12:00 PM 4:00 PM - 7:00 PM 11:00 PM - 2:00 AM
4:30 AM **to** **4:59 AM**	8:30 AM -11:30 AM 3:30 PM - 6:30 PM 10:30 PM - 1:30 AM	5:30 AM - 8:30 AM 12:30 PM - 3:30 PM 7:30 PM - 10:30 PM 2:30 AM - 5:30 AM	9:30 AM - 12:30 PM 4:30 PM - 7:30 PM 11:30 PM - 2:30 AM
5:00 AM **to** **5:29 AM**	9:00 AM -12:00 PM 4:00 PM - 7:00 PM 11:00 PM - 2:00 AM	6:00 AM - 9:00 AM 1:00 PM - 4:00 PM 8:00 PM - 11:00 PM 3:00 AM - 6:00 AM	10:00 AM - 1:00 PM 5:00 PM - 8:00 PM 12:00 AM - 3:00 AM
5:30 AM **to** **5:59 AM**	9:30 AM -12:30 PM 4:30 PM - 7:30 PM 11:30 PM - 2:30 AM	6:30 AM - 9:30 AM 1:30 PM - 4:30 PM 8:30 PM - 11:30 PM 3:30 AM - 6:30 AM	10:30 AM - 1:30 PM 5:30 PM - 8:30 PM 12:30 AM - 3:30 AM

Refer to *Sample Chart* on page *36* for instructions.

PERSONAL LUCK CHART

WEDNESDAY	THURSDAY	FRIDAY	SATURDAY
5:00 AM - 8:00 AM 12:00 PM - 3:00 PM 7:00 PM - 10:00 PM	2:00 AM - 5:00 AM 9:00 AM - 12:00 PM 4:00 PM - 7:00 PM 11:00 PM - 2:00 AM	6:00 AM - 9:00 AM 1:00 PM - 4:00 PM 8:00 PM - 11:00 PM	3:00 AM - 6:00 AM 10:00 AM - 1:00 PM 5:00 PM - 8:00 PM 12:00 AM - 3:00 AM
5:30 AM - 8:30 AM 12:30 PM - 3:30 PM 7:30 PM - 10:30 PM	2:30 AM - 5:30 AM 9:30 AM - 12:30 PM 4:30 PM - 7:30 PM 11:30 PM - 2:30 AM	6:30 AM - 9:30 AM 1:30 PM - 4:30 PM 8:30 PM - 11:30 PM	3:30 AM - 6:30 AM 10:30 AM - 1:30 PM 5:30 PM - 8:30 PM 12:30 AM - 3:30 AM
6:00 AM - 9:00 AM 1:00 PM - 4:00 PM 8:00 PM - 11:00 PM	3:30 AM - 6:00 AM 10:00 AM - 1:00 PM 5:00 PM - 8:00 PM 12:00 AM - 3:00 AM	7:00 AM - 10:00 AM 2:00 PM - 5:00 PM 9:00 PM - 12:00 AM	4:00 AM - 7:00 AM 11:00 AM - 2:00 PM 6:00 PM - 9:00 PM 1:00 AM - 4:00 AM
6:30 AM - 9:30 AM 1:30 PM - 4:30 PM 8:30 PM - 11:30 PM	3:30 AM - 6:30 AM 10:30 AM - 1:30 PM 5:30 PM - 8:30 PM 12:30 AM - 3:30 AM	7:30 AM - 10:30 AM 2:30 PM - 5:30 PM 9:30 PM - 12:30 AM	4:30 AM - 7:30 AM 11:30 AM - 2:30 PM 6:30 PM - 9:30 PM 1:30 AM - 4:30 AM
7:00 AM - 10:00 AM 2:00 PM - 5:00 PM 9:00 PM - 12:00 AM	4:00 AM - 7:00 AM 11:00 AM - 2:00 PM 6:00 PM - 9:00 PM 1:00 AM - 4:00 AM	8:00 AM - 11:00 AM 3:00 PM - 6:00 PM 10:00 PM - 1:00 AM	5:00 AM - 8:00 AM 12:00 PM - 3:00 PM 7:00 PM - 10:00 PM 2:00 AM - 5:00 AM
7:30 AM - 10:30 AM 2:30 PM - 5:30 PM 9:30 PM - 12:30 AM	4:30 AM - 7:30 AM 11:30 AM - 2:30 PM 6:30 PM - 9:30 PM 1:30 AM - 4:30 AM	8:30 AM - 11:30 AM 3:30 PM - 6:30 PM 10:30 PM - 1:30 AM	5:30 AM - 8:30 AM 12:30 PM - 3:30 PM 7:30 PM - 10:30 PM 2:30 AM - 5:30 AM

SUNRISE	SUNDAY	MONDAY	TUESDAY
6:00 AM **to** **6:29 AM**	10:00 AM -1:00 PM 5:00 PM - 8:00 PM 12:00 AM - 3:00 AM	7:00 AM - 10:00 AM 2:00 PM - 5:00 PM 9:00 PM - 12:00 AM 4:00 AM - 7:00 AM	11:00 AM - 2:00 PM 6:00 PM - 9:00 PM 1:00 AM - 4:00 AM
6:30 AM **to** **6:59 AM**	10:30 AM -1:30 PM 5:30 PM - 8:30 PM 12:30 AM - 3:30 AM	7:30 AM - 10:30 AM 2:30 PM - 5:30 PM 9:30 PM - 12:30 AM 4:30 AM - 7:30 AM	11:30 AM - 2:30 PM 6:30 PM - 9:30 PM 1:30 AM - 4:30 AM
7:00 AM **to** **7:29 AM**	11:00 AM - 2:00 PM 6:00 PM - 9:00 PM 1:00 AM - 4:00 AM	8:00 AM - 11:00 AM 3:00 PM - 6:00 PM 10:00 PM - 1:00 AM 5:00 AM - 8:00 AM	5:00 AM - 8:00 AM 12:00 PM - 3:00 PM 7:00 PM - 10:00 PM 2:00 AM - 5:00 AM
7:30 AM **to** **7:59 AM**	11:30 AM - 2:30 PM 6:30 PM - 9:30 PM 1:30 AM - 4:30 AM	8:30 AM - 11:30 AM 3:30 PM - 6:30 PM 10:30 PM - 1:30 AM 5:30 AM - 8:30 AM	5:30 AM - 8:30 AM 12:30 PM - 3:30 PM 7:30 PM - 10:30 PM 2:30 AM - 5:30 AM
8:00 AM **to** **8:29 AM**	12:00 PM - 3:00 PM 7:00 PM - 10:00 PM 2:00 AM - 5:00 AM	9:00 AM - 12:00 PM 4:00 PM - 7:00 PM 11:00 PM - 2:00 AM	6:00 AM - 9:00 AM 1:00 PM - 4:00 PM 8:00 PM - 11:00 PM 3:00 AM - 6:00 AM
8:30 AM **to** **8:59 AM**	12:30 PM - 3:30 PM 7:30 PM - 10:30 PM 2:30 AM - 5:30 AM	9:30 AM - 12:30 PM 4:30 PM - 7:30 PM 11:30 PM - 2:30 AM	6:30 AM - 9:30 AM 1:30 PM - 4:30 PM 8:30 PM - 11:30 PM 3:30 AM - 6:30 AM

WEDNESDAY	THURSDAY	FRIDAY	SATURDAY
8:00 AM - 11:00 AM 3:00 PM - 6:00 PM 10:00 PM - 1:00 AM	5:00 AM - 8:00 AM 12:00 AM - 3:00 PM 7:00 PM - 10:00 PM 2:00 AM - 5:00 AM	9:00 AM - 12:00 PM 4:00 PM -7:00 PM 11:00 PM - 2:00 AM	6:00 AM -9:00 AM 1:00 PM - 4:00 PM 8:00 PM -11:00 PM 3:00 AM - 6:00 AM
8:30 AM - 11:30 AM 3:30 PM - 6:30 PM 10:30 PM - 1:30 AM	5:30 AM - 8:30 AM 12:30 PM - 3:30 PM 7:30 PM - 10:30 PM 2:30 AM - 5:30 AM	9:30 AM - 12:30 PM 4:30 PM - 7:30 PM 11:30 PM - 2:30 AM	6:30 AM - 9:30 AM 1:30 PM - 4:30 PM 8:30 PM - 11:30 PM 3:30 AM - 6:30 AM
9:00 AM - 12:00 PM 4:00 PM - 7:00 PM 11:00 PM - 2:00 AM	6:00 AM - 9:00 AM 1:00 PM - 4:00 PM 8:00 PM - 11:00 PM 3:00 AM - 6:00 AM	10:00 AM - 1:00 PM 5:00 PM - 8:00 PM 12:00 AM - 3:00 AM	7:00 AM - 10:00 AM 2:00 PM - 5:00 PM 9:00 PM - 12:00 AM 4:00 AM - 7:00 AM
9:30 AM - 12:30 AM 4:30 PM - 7:30 PM 11:30 PM - 2:30 AM	6:30 AM - 9:30 AM 1:30 PM - 4:30 PM 8:30 PM - 11:30 PM 3:30 AM - 6:30 AM	10:30 AM - 1:30 PM 5:30 PM - 8:30 PM 12:30 AM - 3:30 AM	7:30 AM - 10:30 AM 2:30 PM - 5:30 PM 9:30 PM - 12:30 AM 4:30 AM - 7:30 AM
10:00 AM - 1:00 PM 5:00 PM - 8:00 PM 12:00 AM - 3:00 AM	7:00 AM - 10:00 AM 2:00 PM - 5:00 PM 9:00 PM - 12:00 AM 4:00 AM - 7:00 AM	11:00 AM - 2:00 PM 6:00 PM - 9:00 PM 1:00 AM - 4:00 AM	8:00 AM - 11:00 AM 3:00 PM - 6:00 PM 10:00 PM - 1:00 AM 5:00 AM - 8:00 AM
10:30 AM - 1:30 PM 5:30 PM - 8:30 PM 12:30 AM - 3:30 AM	7:30 AM - 10:30 AM 2:30 AM - 5:30 AM 9:30 PM - 12:30 AM 4:30 AM - 7:30 AM	11:30 AM - 2:30 PM 6:30 PM - 9:30 PM 1:30 AM - 4:30 AM	8:30 AM - 11:30 AM 3:30 PM - 6:30 PM 10:30 PM - 1:30 AM 5:30 AM - 8:30 AM

CAPRICORN

There is no getting away from the fact, that there are only nine numbers by which all our calculations on earth are made. Beyond these nine numbers, all the rest are repetition, as 10 is a 1 with a 0 added, eleven (11) is 1+1=2; and so on. Every number, no matter how high, can be reduced to a single figure. This is why your lucky numbers first appear as single numbers, followed by numbers adding up to this single number, up to 31. However, any number over 31 which adds up to any of your single lucky numbers, is also lucky for you.

Your first lucky number is - 2 - and all numbers adding up to 2, such as 11-20-29 - Lucky day Monday. This number was determined by combining your celestial number with other factors of your sun sign.

Your luckiest number is 2. Bear this in mind at all times. When you buy a ticket of any sort, make sure that the serial number has the predominant number 2 in it, and buy it during one of your lucky periods. Also a street address containing one or more 2's; horse number 2, player number 2 in a game; a 2 rolled in dice; room number 2 in a hotel/motel; and so on. These

are all considered fortunate for you. You can also combine number 2 with your other lucky numbers.

Your second lucky number is your birth date.

Your third lucky number is - 8 - as well as 17 and 26 - Lucky day Saturday. This is the number assigned to the planet Saturn, ruler of Capricorn.

BIRTH DATES

NUMBERS: 1 - 10 - 19 - 28
LUCKY DAYS: Sunday and Monday.

People born on one of these dates are fortunate, because these numbers are related to 4-13-22-31 (lucky day Sunday), and the series of 1 and 4 are interrelated to 2-11-20-29 and 7-16-25 (lucky day Monday). Therefore, all these numbers are especially lucky on Sunday and Monday.

Your lucky yearly periods are; July 20th to August 28th and March 21st to April 28th.

NUMBERS: 2 - 11 - 20 - 29
LUCKY DAYS: Monday and Sunday.

If one of these dates is your birth date, these numbers are extremely lucky for you, since they happen to be the same as your first lucky number.

People born on one of these dates are fortunate, because these numbers are related to 7-16-25 (lucky day Monday), and the series of 2 and 7 are interrelated to 1-10-19-28 and 4-13-22-31 (lucky day Sunday). Therefore, all these numbers are especially lucky on Monday and Sunday.

Your lucky yearly period is from June 21st to July 27th.

NUMBERS: 3 - 12 - 21 - 30
LUCKY DAY: Thursday

NOTE: Since these numbers are part of the 3-6-9 combination, you will have a certain degree of luck with 6-15-24 (lucky day Friday) and 9-18-27 (lucky day Tuesday). All these numbers are especially lucky on Thursday, Tuesday and Friday.

Your lucky yearly periods are; February 19th to March 27th and November 21st to December 27th.

NUMBERS: 4 - 13 - 22 - 31
LUCKY DAYS: Sunday and Monday

People born on one of these dates are fortunate, because these numbers are related to 1-10-19-28 (lucky day Sunday), and the series of 4 and 1 are interrelated to 2-11-20-29 and 7-16-25 (lucky day Monday). Therefore, all these numbers are especially lucky on Sunday and Monday.

Your lucky yearly period is from June 21st to August 30th.

NUMBERS: 5 - 14 - 23
LUCKY DAY: Wednesday

You will also have a certain degree of luck on Fridays.

Your lucky yearly periods are; May 21st to June 27th and August 21st to September 27th.

NUMBERS: 6 - 15 - 24
LUCKY DAY: Friday

NOTE: Since these numbers are part of the 3-6-9 combination, you will have a certain degree of luck with 3-12-21-30 (lucky day Thursday) and 9-18-27 (lucky day Tuesday). All these numbers are especially lucky on Friday, Tuesday and Thursday.

Your lucky yearly periods are; April 20th to May 27th and September 21st to October 27th.

NUMBERS: 7 - 16 - 25
LUCKY DAYS: Monday and Sunday

People born on one of these dates are fortunate, because these numbers are related to 2-11-20-29 (lucky day Monday), and the series of 7 and 2 are interrelated to 1-10-19-28 and 4-13-22-31 (lucky day Sunday). Therefore, all these numbers are especially lucky on Monday and Sunday.

Your lucky yearly period is from June 21st to July 27th, and less strongly from this date to the end of August.

NUMBERS: 8 - 17 - 26
LUCKY DAY: Saturday

If one of these dates is your birth date, these numbers are extremely lucky for you, since they happen to be the same as your third lucky number.

Since number 8 has a connection to number 4, you could have a certain degree of luck on Sundays.

Your lucky yearly periods are; from December 21st to December 31st, all of January up to February 26th.

NUMBERS: 9 - 18 - 27
LUCKY DAY: Tuesday

NOTE: Since these numbers are part of the 3-6-9 combination, you will have a certain degree of luck with 3-12-21-30 (lucky day Thursday) and 6-15-24 (lucky day Friday). All these numbers are especially lucky on Tuesday, Thursday and Friday.

Your lucky yearly periods are; March 21st to April 27th and October 21st to November 27th.

DECANS

Note: Decans are Stars or Constellations that rise once every ten days and by which the ancient Egyptians used to tell time.

There are certain periods during the year that are most fortunate for you, when your chances of winning are amplified even more.

If you were born on December 22, 23, 24, 25, 26, 27, 28, 29, 30, 31 - the following periods are lucky for you.

February 20th to 29th
April 21st to May 2nd
August 23rd to September 3rd
✓October 22nd to November 2nd

If you were born on January 1, 2, 3, 4, 5, 6, 7, 8, 9, 10 - the following periods are lucky for you.

March 1st to March 10th
May 2nd to 12th
September 4th to 14th
November 2nd to 12th

If you were born on January 11, 12, 13, 14, 15, 16, 17, 18, 19, 20 - the following periods are lucky for you.

March 10th to 20th
May 11th to 21st
September 13th to 24th
November 13th to 22nd

The lucky periods in your Personal Luck Chart, and your lucky numbers, remain the same for the rest of your life. They are based on your birth date and the time of sunrise, which varies greatly throughout the year. I have provided you with sunrise times from 3:00 a.m. to 9:00 a.m.. Your lucky hours have been indicated for each hour of sunrise, for each day of the week. The only thing that changes is the time of sunrise, so all you have to do is check the sunrise time on any given day of the year, and go by the lucky hours listed for that time and day. For this reason, it doesn't matter if it's standard or daylight savings time. It also doesn't matter if you are at home or in another part of the world. Just go by the sunrise time for the location you are in, to determine your lucky hours.

Refer to *Sample Chart* on page *36* for instructions.

CAPRICORN PERSONAL

SUNRISE	SUNDAY	MONDAY	TUESDAY
3:00 AM to **3:29 AM**	6:00 AM - 9:00 AM 1:00 PM - 4:00 PM 8:00 PM - 11:00 PM	3:00 AM - 6:00 AM 10:00 AM - 1:00 PM 5:00 PM - 8:00 PM 12:00 AM - 3:00 AM	7:00 AM - 10:00 AM 2:00 PM - 5:00 PM 9:00 PM - 12:00 AM
3:30 AM to **3:59 AM**	6:30 AM - 9:30 AM 1:30 PM - 4:30 PM 8:30 PM - 11:30 PM	3:30 AM - 6:30 AM 10:30 AM - 1:30 PM 5:30 PM - 8:30 PM 12:30 AM - 3:30 AM	7:30 AM - 10:30 AM 2:30 PM - 5:30 PM 9:30 PM - 12:30 AM
4:00 AM to **4:29 AM**	7:00 AM - 10:00 AM 2:00 PM - 5:00 PM 9:00 PM - 12:00 AM	4:00 AM -7:00 AM 11:00 AM - 2:00 PM 6:00 PM - 9:00 PM 1:00 AM - 4:00 AM	8:00 AM - 11:00 AM 3:00 PM - 6:00 PM 10:00 PM - 1:00 AM
4:30 AM to **4:59 AM**	7:30 AM - 10:30 AM 2:30 PM - 5:30 PM 9:30 PM - 12:30 AM	4:30 AM -7:30 AM 11:30 AM - 2:30 PM 6:30 PM - 9:30 PM 1:30 AM - 4:30 AM	8:30 AM - 11:30 AM 3:30 PM - 6:30 PM 10:30 PM - 1:30 AM
5:00 AM to **5:29 AM**	8:00 AM - 11:00 AM 3:00 PM - 6:00 PM 10:00 PM - 1:00 AM	5:00 AM - 8:00 AM 12:00 PM - 3:00 PM 7:00 PM - 10:00 PM 2:00 AM - 5:00 AM	9:00 AM - 12:00 PM 4:00 PM - 7:00 PM 11:00 PM - 2:00 AM
5:30 AM to **5:59 AM**	8:30 AM - 11:30 AM 3:30 PM - 6:30 PM 10:30 PM - 1:30 AM	5:30 AM - 8:30 AM 12:30 PM - 3:30 PM 7:30 PM - 10:30 PM 2:30 AM - 5:30 AM	9:30 AM - 12:30 PM 4:30 PM -7:30 PM 11:30 PM - 2:30 AM

Refer to *Sample Chart* on page *36* for instructions.

LUCK CHART

WEDNESDAY	THURSDAY	FRIDAY	SATURDAY
4:00 AM - 7:00 AM 11:00 AM - 2:00 PM 6:00 PM - 9:00 PM 1:00 AM - 4:00 AM	8:00 AM - 11:00 AM 3:00 PM - 6:00 PM 10:00 PM - 1:00 AM	5:00 AM - 8:00 AM 12:00 PM - 3:00 PM 7:00 PM - 10:00 PM	2:00 AM - 5:00 AM 9:00 AM - 12:00 AM 4:00 PM - 7:00 PM 11:00 PM - 2:00 AM
4:30 AM - 7:30 AM 11:30 AM - 2:30 PM 6:30 PM - 9:30 PM 1:30 AM - 4:30 AM	8:30 AM - 11:30 AM 3:30 PM - 6:30 PM 10:30 PM - 1:30 AM	5:30 AM - 8:30 AM 12:30 PM - 3:30 PM 7:30 PM - 10:30 PM	2:30 AM - 5:30 AM 9:30 AM - 12:30 PM 4:30 PM - 7:30 PM 11:30 PM - 2:30 AM
5:00 AM - 8:00 AM 12:00 PM - 3:00 PM 7:00 PM - 10:00 PM 2:00 AM - 5:00 AM	9:00 AM - 12:00 PM 4:00 PM - 7:00 PM 11:00 PM - 2:00 AM	6:00 AM - 9:00 AM 1:00 PM - 4:00 PM 8:00 PM - 11:00 PM	3:00 AM - 6:00 AM 10:00 AM - 1:00 PM 5:00 PM - 8:00 PM 12:00 PM - 3:00 AM
5:30 AM - 8:30 AM 12:30 PM - 3:30 PM 7:30 PM - 10:30 PM 2:30 AM - 5:30 AM	9:30 AM - 12:30 PM 4:30 PM - 7:30 PM 11:30 PM - 2:30 AM	6:30 AM -9:30 AM 1:30 PM - 4:30 PM 8:30 PM - 11:30 PM	3:30 AM - 6:30 AM 10:30 AM - 1:30 PM 5:30 PM - 8:30 PM 12:30 AM - 3:30 AM
6:00 AM - 9:00 AM 1:00 PM - 4:00 PM 8:00 PM - 11:00 PM 3:00 AM - 6:00 AM	10:00 AM - 1:00 PM 5:00 PM - 8:00 PM 12:00 PM - 3:00 AM	7:00 AM - 10:00 AM 2:00 PM - 5:00 PM 9:00 PM - 12:00 AM	4:00 AM - 7:00 AM 11:00 AM - 2:00 PM 6:00 PM - 9:00 PM 1:00 AM - 4:00 AM
6:30 AM -9:30 AM 1:30 PM - 4:30 PM 8:30 PM - 11:30 PM 3:30 AM - 6:30 AM	10:30 AM - 1:30 PM 5:30 PM - 8:30 PM 12:30 AM - 3:30 AM	7:30 AM - 10:30 AM 2:30 PM - 5:30 PM 9:30 PM - 12:30 AM	4:30 AM - 7:30 AM 11:30 AM - 2:30 PM 6:30 PM -9:30 PM 1:30 AM - 4:30 AM

SUNRISE	SUNDAY	MONDAY	TUESDAY
6:00 AM **to** **6:29 AM**	9:00 AM -12:00 PM 4:00 PM - 7:00 PM 11:00 PM - 2:00 AM	6:00 AM - 9:00 AM 1:00 PM - 4:00 PM 8:00 PM - 11:00 PM 3:00 AM - 6:00 AM	10:00 AM - 1:00 PM 5:00 PM - 8:00 PM 12:00 AM - 3:00 AM
6:30 AM **to** **6:59 AM**	9:30 AM - 12:30 PM 4:30 PM - 7:30 PM 11:30 PM - 2:30 AM	6:30 AM - 9:30 AM 1:30 PM - 4:30 PM 8:30 PM - 11:30 PM 3:30 AM - 6:30 AM	10:30 AM - 1:30 PM 5:30 PM - 8:30 PM 12:30 AM - 3:30 AM
7:00 AM **to** **7:29 AM**	10:00 AM -1:00 PM 5:00 PM - 8:00 PM 12:00 AM - 3:00 AM	7:00 AM - 10:00 AM 2:00 PM - 5:00 PM 9:00 PM - 12:00 AM	4:00 AM - 7:00 AM 11:00 AM - 2:00 PM 6:00 PM - 9:00 PM 1:00 AM - 4:00 AM
7:30 AM **to** **7:59 AM**	10:30 AM -1:30 PM 5:30 PM - 8:30 PM 12:30 AM - 3:30 AM	7:30 AM - 10:30 AM 2:30 PM - 5:30 PM 9:30 PM - 12:30 AM	4:30 AM - 7:30 AM 11:30 AM - 2:30 PM 6:30 PM - 9:30 PM 1:30 AM - 4:30 AM
8:00 AM **to** **8:29 AM**	11:00 AM - 2:00 PM 6:00 PM - 9:00 PM 1:00 AM - 4:00 AM	8:00 AM - 11:00 AM 3:00 PM - 6:00 PM 10:00 PM - 1:00 AM	5:00 AM - 8:00 AM 12:00 PM - 3:00 PM 7:00 PM - 10:00 PM 2:00 AM - 5:00 AM
8:30 AM **to** **8:59 AM**	11:30 AM - 2:30 PM 6:30 PM - 9:30 PM 1:30 AM - 4:30 AM	8:30 AM - 11:30 AM 3:30 PM - 6:30 PM 10:30 PM - 1:30 AM	5:30 AM - 8:30 AM 12:30 PM - 3:30 PM 7:30 PM - 10:30 PM 2:30 AM - 5:30 AM

WEDNESDAY	THURSDAY	FRIDAY	SATURDAY
7:00 AM - 10:00 AM 2:00 PM - 5:00 PM 9:00 PM - 12:00 AM 4:00 AM - 7:00 AM	11:00 AM - 2:00 PM 6:00 PM - 9:00 PM 1:00 AM - 4:00 AM	8:00 AM - 11:00 AM 3:00 PM - 6:00 PM 10:00 PM - 1:00 AM	5:00 AM - 8:00 AM 12:00 PM - 3:00 PM 7:00 PM - 10:00 AM 2:00 AM - 5:00 AM
7:30 AM - 10:30 AM 2:30 PM - 5:30 PM 9:30 PM - 12:30 AM 4:30 AM - 7:30 AM	11:30 AM - 2:30 PM 6:30 PM - 9:30 PM 1:30 AM - 4:30 AM	8:30 AM - 11:30 AM 3:30 PM - 6:30 PM 10:30 PM - 1:30 AM	5:30 AM - 8:30 AM 12:30 PM - 3:30 PM 7:30 PM - 10:30 AM 2:30 AM - 5:30 AM
8:00 AM - 11:00 AM 3:00 PM - 6:00 PM 10:00 PM - 1:00 AM	5:00 AM - 8:00 AM 12:00 PM - 3:00 PM 7:00 PM - 10:00 PM 2:00 AM - 5:00 AM	9:00 AM - 12:00 PM 4:00 PM - 7:00 PM 11:00 PM - 2:00 AM	6:00 AM - 9:00 AM 1:00 PM - 4:00 PM 8:00 PM -11:00 AM 3:00 AM - 6:00 AM
8:30 AM - 11:30 AM 3:30 PM - 6:30 PM 10:30 PM - 1:30 AM	5:30 AM - 8:30 AM 12:30 PM - 3:30 PM 7:30 PM - 10:30 PM 2:30 AM - 5:30 AM	9:30 AM - 12:30 PM 4:30 PM - 7:30 PM 11:30 PM - 2:30 AM	6:30 AM - 9:30 AM 1:30 PM - 4:30 PM 8:30 PM - 11:30 AM 3:30 AM - 6:30 AM
9:00 AM - 12:00 PM 4:00 PM - 7:00 PM 11:00 PM - 2:00 AM	6:00 AM - 9:00 AM 1:00 PM - 4:00 PM 8:00 PM -11:00 AM 3:00 AM - 6:00 AM	10:00 AM - 1:00 PM 5:00 PM - 8:00 PM 12:00 AM - 3:00 AM	7:00 AM - 10:00 AM 2:00 PM - 5:00 PM 9:00 PM - 12:00 PM 4:00 AM - 7:00 AM
9:30 AM - 12:30 PM 4:30 PM - 7:30 PM 11:30 PM - 2:30 AM	6:30 AM - 9:30 AM 1:30 PM - 4:30 PM 8:30 PM - 11:30 PM 3:30 AM - 6:30 AM	10:30 AM - 1:30 PM 5:30 PM - 8:30 PM 12:30 AM - 3:30 AM	7:30 AM - 10:30 AM 2:30 PM - 5:30 PM 9:30 PM - 12:30 PM 4:30 AM - 7:30 AM

AQUARIUS

There is no getting away from the fact, that there are only nine numbers by which our calculations on this earth are made. Beyond these nine numbers, all the rest are repetition, as 10 is a 1 with a 0 added, eleven (11) 1+1=2; and so on. Every number, no matter how high, can be reduced to a single figure. This is why your lucky numbers first appear as single numbers, followed by numbers adding up to this single number, up to 31. However, any number over 31 which adds up to any of your single numbers, is also lucky for you.

Your first lucky number is - 3 - and all numbers adding up to 3, such as 12-21-30 - Lucky day Thursday. This number was determined by combining your celestial number with other factors of your sun sign.

Your luckiest number is 3. Bear this in mind at all times. When you buy a ticket of any sort, make sure that the serial number has the predominant number 3 in it, and buy it during one of your lucky periods. Also a street address containing one or more 3's; horse number 3, player number 3 in a game; a 3 rolled in dice; room number 3 in a hotel/motel; and so on. These are all considered fortunate for you. You can also combine number 3 with your other lucky numbers.

Your second lucky number is your birth date.

Your third lucky number is - 4 - as well as 13-22-31.

Lucky day Sunday and Saturday. This is the number assigned to
the planet Uranus, ruler of Aquarius. Since the planet Saturn is
co-ruler of Aquarius, you will also have a certain degree of luck
with number - 8 - (17-26), lucky day Saturday.

BIRTH DATES

NUMBERS: 1 - 10 - 19 - 28
LUCKY DAYS: Sunday and Monday
     People born on one of these dates are fortunate, because
these numbers are related to 4-13-22-31 (lucky day Sunday), and
the series of 1 and 4 are interrelated to 2-11-20-29 and 7-16-25
(lucky day Monday). Therefore, all these numbers are especially
lucky on Sunday and Monday.
     Your lucky yearly periods are; July 20th to August 28th
and March 21st to April 28th.

NUMBERS: 2 - 11 - 20 - 29
LUCKY DAYS: Monday and Sunday
     People born on one of these dates are fortunate, because
these numbers are related to 7-16-25 (lucky day Monday), and the
series of 2 and 7 are interrelated to 1-10-19-28 and 4-13-22-31
(lucky day Sunday). Therefore, all these numbers are especially
lucky on Monday and Sunday.
     Your lucky yearly period is from June 21st to July 27th.

NUMBERS: 3 - 12 - 21 - 30
LUCKY DAY: Thursday
     If one of these dates is your birth date, these numbers are
extremely lucky for you, since they happen to be the same as your
first lucky number.
     NOTE: Since these numbers are part of the 3-6-9
combination, you will have a certain degree of luck with 6-15-24
(lucky day Friday) and 9-18-27 (lucky day Tuesday). All these
numbers are especially lucky on Thursday, Tuesday and Friday.
     Your lucky yearly periods are; February 19th to March
27th and November 21st to December 27th.

NUMBERS: 4 - 13 - 22 - 31
LUCKY DAYS: Sunday and Monday

People born on one of these dates are fortunate, because these numbers are related to 1-10-19-28 (lucky day Sunday), and the series of 4 and 1 are interrelated to 2-11-20-29 and 7-16-25 (lucky day Monday). Therefore, all these numbers are especially lucky on Sunday and Monday.

Your lucky yearly period is from June 21st to August 30th.

NUMBERS: 5 - 14 - 23
LUCKY DAY: Wednesday

You will also have a certain degree of luck on Fridays.

Your lucky yearly periods are; May 21st to June 27th and August 21st to September 27th.

NUMBERS: 6 - 15 - 24
LUCKY DAY: Friday

NOTE: Since these numbers are part of the 3-6-9 combination, you will have a certain degree of luck with 3-12-21-30 (lucky day Thursday) and 9-18-27 (lucky day Tuesday). All these numbers are especially lucky on Friday, Tuesday and Thursday.

Your lucky yearly periods are; April 20th to May 27th and September 21st to October 27th.

NUMBERS: 7 - 16 - 25
LUCKY DAYS: Monday and Sunday

People born on one of these dates are fortunate, because these numbers are related to 2-11-20-29 (lucky day Monday), and the series of 7 and 2 are interrelated to 1-10-19-28 and 4-13-22-31 (lucky day Sunday). Therefore, all these numbers are especially lucky on Monday and Sunday.

Your lucky yearly period is from June 21st to July 27th, and less strongly from this date to the end of August.

NUMBERS: 8 - 17 - 26
LUCKY DAY: SATURDAY
     If one of these dates is your birth date, these numbers are extremely lucky for you, since they happen to be the same as your third lucky number. Since number 8 has a connection to number 4, you could have a certain degree of luck on Sundays.
     Your lucky yearly periods are; from December 21st to December 31st, all of January up to February 26th.

NUMBERS: 9 - 18 - 27
LUCKY DAY: Tuesday
     NOTE: Since these numbers are part of the 3-6-9 combination, you will have a certain degree of luck with 3-12-21-30 (lucky day Thursday) and 6-15-24 (lucky day Friday). All these numbers are especially lucky on Tuesday, Thursday and Friday.
     Your lucky yearly periods are; March 21st to April 27th and October 21st to November 27th.

DECANS
     Note: Decans are Stars or Constellations that rise once every ten days and by which the ancient Egyptians used to tell time.

     There are certain periods during the year that are most fortunate for you, when your chances of winning are amplified even more.

     If you were born on January 21, 22, 23, 24, 25, 26, 27, 28, 29, 30 - the following periods are lucky for you.
               March 21st to 31st
               May 22nd to June 2nd
               September 24th to October 4th
               November 24th to December 4th

If you were born on January 31 or February 1, 2, 3, 4, 5, 6, 7, 8, 9 - the following periods are lucky for you.

April 1st to 12th
June 1st to 11th
October 3rd to 13th
December 3rd to 13th

If you were born on February 10, 11, 12, 13, 14, 15, 16, 17, 18, 19 - the following periods are lucky for you.

April 11th to 20th
June 11th to 21st
October 13th to 23rd
December 11th to 22nd

The lucky periods in your Personal Luck Chart, and your lucky numbers, remain the same for the rest of your life. They are based on your birth date and the time of sunrise, which varies greatly throughout the year. I have provided you with sunrise times from 3:00 a.m. to 9:00 a.m.. Your lucky hours have been indicated for each hour of sunrise, for each day of the week. The only thing that changes is the time of sunrise, so all you have to do is check the sunrise time on any given day of the year, and go by the lucky hours listed for that time and day. For this reason, it doesn't matter if it's standard or daylight savings time. It also doesn't matter if you are at home or in another part of the world. Just go by the sunrise time for the location you are in, to determine your lucky hours.

Refer to *Sample Chart* on page *36* for instructions.

AQUARIUS PERSONAL

SUNRISE	SUNDAY	MONDAY	TUESDAY
3:00 AM **to** **3:29 AM**	4:00 AM - 7:00 AM 11:00 AM - 2:00 PM 6:00 PM - 9:00 PM 1:00 AM - 4:00 AM	8:00 AM - 11:00 AM 3:00 PM - 6:00 PM 10:00 PM - 1:00 AM	5:00 AM - 8:00 AM 12:00 PM - 3:00 PM 7:00 PM - 10:00 PM
3:30 AM **to** **3:59 AM**	4:30 AM - 7:30 AM 11:30 AM - 2:30 PM 6:30 PM - 9:30 PM 1:30 AM - 4:30 AM	8:30 AM - 11:30 AM 3:30 PM - 6:30 PM 10:30 PM - 1:30 AM	5:30 AM - 8:30 AM 12:30 PM - 3:30 PM 7:30 PM - 10:30 PM
4:00 AM **to** **4:29 AM**	5:00 AM - 8:00 AM 12:00 PM - 3:00 PM 7:00 PM - 10:00 PM 2:00 AM - 5:00 AM	9:00 AM - 12:00 PM 4:00 PM - 7:00 PM 11:00 PM - 2:00 AM	6:00 AM - 9:00 AM 1:00 PM - 4:00 PM 8:00 PM - 11:00 PM
4:30 AM **to** **4:59 AM**	5:30 AM - 8:30 AM 12:30 PM - 3:30 PM 7:30 PM - 10:30 PM 2:30 AM - 5:30 AM	9:30 AM - 12:30 PM 4:30 PM - 7:30 PM 11:30 PM - 2:30 AM	6:30 AM - 9:30 AM 1:30 PM - 4:30 PM 8:30 PM - 11:30 PM
5:00 AM **to** **5:29 AM**	6:00 AM - 9:00 AM 1:00 PM - 4:00 PM 8:00 PM - 11:00 PM 3:00 AM - 6:00 AM	10:00 AM - 1:00 PM 5:00 PM - 8:00 PM 12:00 AM - 3:00 AM	7:00 AM -10:00 AM 2:00 PM - 5:00 PM 9:00 PM - 12:00 AM
5:30 AM **to** **5:59 AM**	6:30 AM - 9:30 AM 1:30 PM - 4:30 PM 8:30 PM - 11:30 PM 3:30 AM - 6:30 AM	10:30 AM - 1:30 PM 5:30 PM - 8:30 PM 12:30 AM - 3:30 AM	7:30 AM -10:30 AM 2:30 PM - 5:30 PM 9:30 PM - 12:30 AM

Refer to *Sample Chart* on page *36* for instructions.

LUCK CHART

WEDNESDAY	THURSDAY	FRIDAY	SATURDAY
2:00 AM - 5:00 AM 9:00 AM - 12:00 PM 4:00 PM - 7:00 PM 11:00 PM - 2:00 AM	6:00 AM - 9:00 AM 1:00 PM - 4:00 PM 8:00 PM - 11:00 PM	3:00 AM - 6:00 AM 10:00 AM - 1:00 PM 5:00 PM - 8:00 PM 12:00 AM - 3:00 AM	7:00 AM - 10:00 AM 2:00 PM - 5:00 PM 9:00 PM -12:00 AM
2:30 AM - 5:30 AM 9:30 AM - 12:30 PM 4:30 PM - 7:30 PM 11:30 PM - 2:30 AM	6:30 AM - 9:30 AM 1:30 PM - 4:30 PM 8:30 PM - 11:30 PM	3:30 AM - 6:30 AM 10:30 AM - 1:30 PM 5:30 PM - 8:30 PM 12:30 AM - 3:30 AM	7:30 AM - 10:30 AM 2:30 PM - 5:30 PM 9:30 PM - 12:30 AM
3:30 AM - 6:00 AM 10:00 AM - 1:00 PM 5:00 PM - 8:00 PM 12:00 AM - 3:00 AM	7:00 AM - 10:00 AM 2:00 PM - 5:00 PM 9:00 PM - 12:00 AM	4:00 AM - 7:00 AM 11:00 AM - 2:00 PM 6:00 PM - 9:00 PM 1:00 AM - 4:00 AM	8:00 AM - 11:00 AM 3:00 PM - 6:00 PM 10:00 PM - 1:00 AM
3:30 AM - 6:30 AM 10:30 AM - 1:30 PM 5:30 PM - 8:30 PM 12:30 AM - 3:30 AM	7:30 AM - 10:30 AM 2:30 PM - 5:30 PM 9:30 PM - 12:30 AM	4:30 AM - 7:30 AM 11:30 AM - 2:30 PM 6:30 PM - 9:30 PM 1:30 AM - 4:30 AM	8:30 AM -11:30 AM 3:30 PM - 6:30 PM 10:30 PM - 1:30 AM
4:00 AM - 7:00 AM 11:00 AM - 2:00 PM 6:00 PM - 9:00 PM 1:00 AM - 4:00 AM	8:00 AM - 11:00 AM 3:00 PM - 6:00 PM 10:00 PM - 1:00 AM	5:00 AM - 8:00 AM 12:00 PM - 3:00 PM 7:00 PM - 10:00 PM 2:00 AM - 5:00 AM	9:00 AM -12:00 PM 4:00 PM - 7:00 PM 11:00 PM - 2:00 AM
4:30 AM - 7:30 AM 11:30 AM - 2:30 PM 6:30 PM - 9:30 PM 1:30 AM - 4:30 AM	8:30 AM - 11:30 AM 3:30 PM - 6:30 PM 10:30 PM - 1:30 AM	5:30 AM - 8:30 AM 12:30 PM - 3:30 PM 7:30 PM - 10:30 PM 2:30 AM - 5:30 AM	9:30 AM -12:30 PM 4:30 PM - 7:30 PM 11:30 PM - 2:30 AM

SUNRISE	SUNDAY	MONDAY	TUESDAY
6:00 AM **to** **6:29 AM**	7:00 AM - 10:00 AM 2:00 PM - 5:00 PM 9:00 PM - 12:00 AM 4:00 AM - 7:00 AM	11:00 AM - 2:00 PM 6:00 PM - 9:00 PM 1:00 AM - 4:00 AM	8:00 AM - 11:00 AM 3:00 PM - 6:00 PM 10:00 PM - 1:00 AM
6:30 AM **to** **6:59 AM**	7:30 AM - 10:30 AM 2:30 PM - 5:30 PM 9:30 PM - 12:30 AM 4:30 AM - 7:30 AM	11:30 AM - 2:30 PM 6:30 PM - 9:30 PM 1:30 AM - 4:30 AM	8:30 AM - 11:30 AM 3:30 PM - 6:30 PM 10:30 PM - 1:30 AM
7:00 AM **to** **7:29 AM**	8:00 AM - 11:00 AM 3:00 PM - 6:00 PM 10:00 PM - 1:00 AM	4:00 AM - 7:00 AM 12:00 PM - 3:00 PM 7:00 PM - 10:00 PM 2:00 AM - 5:00 AM	9:00 AM - 12:00 PM 4:00 PM - 7:00 PM 11:00 PM - 2:00 AM
7:30 AM **to** **7:59 AM**	8:30 AM - 11:30 AM 3:30 PM - 6:30 PM 10:30 PM - 1:30 AM	4:30 AM - 7:30 AM 12:30 PM - 3:30 PM 7:30 PM - 10:30 PM 2:30 AM - 5:30 AM	9:30 AM - 12:30 PM 4:30 PM - 7:30 PM 11:30 PM - 2:30 AM
8:00 AM **to** **8:29 AM**	9:00 AM - 12:00 PM 4:00 PM - 7:00 PM 11:00 PM - 2:00 AM	5:00 AM - 8:00 AM 1:00 PM - 4:00 PM 8:00 PM - 11:00 PM 3:00 AM - 6:00 AM	10:00 AM -1:00 PM 5:00 PM - 8:00 PM 12:00 AM - 3:00 AM
8:30 AM **to** **8:59 AM**	9:30 AM - 12:30 PM 4:30 PM - 7:30 PM 11:30 PM - 2:30 AM	5:30 AM - 8:30 AM 1:30 PM - 4:30 PM 8:30 PM - 11:30 PM 3:30 AM - 6:30 AM	10:30 AM -1:30 PM 5:30 PM - 8:30 PM 12:30 AM - 3:30 AM

WEDNESDAY	THURSDAY	FRIDAY	SATURDAY
5:00 AM - 8:00 AM 12:00 AM - 3:00 PM 7:00 PM - 10:00 PM 2:00 AM - 5:00 AM	9:00 AM - 12:00 PM 4:00 PM -7:00 PM 11:00 PM - 2:00 AM	6:00 AM -9:00 AM 1:00 PM - 4:00 PM 8:00 PM -11:00 PM 3:00 AM - 6:00 AM	10:00 AM - 1:00 PM 5:00 PM - 8:00 PM 12:00 AM -3:00 AM
5:30 AM - 8:30 AM 12:30 PM - 3:30 PM 7:30 PM - 10:30 PM 2:30 AM - 5:30 AM	9:30 AM - 12:30 PM 4:30 PM - 7:30 PM 11:30 PM - 2:30 AM	6:30 AM - 9:30 AM 1:30 PM - 4:30 PM 8:30 PM - 11:30 PM 3:30 AM - 6:30 AM	10:30 AM - 1:30 PM 5:30 PM - 8:30 PM 12:30 AM - 3:30 AM
6:00 AM - 9:00 AM 1:00 PM - 4:00 PM 8:00 PM - 11:00 PM 3:00 AM - 6:00 AM	10:00 AM - 1:00 PM 5:00 PM - 8:00 PM 12:00 AM - 3:00 AM	7:00 AM - 10:00 AM 2:00 PM - 5:00 PM 9:00 PM - 12:00 AM 4:00 AM - 7:00 AM	11:00 AM - 2:00 PM 6:00 PM - 9:00 PM 1:00 AM - 4:00 AM
6:30 AM - 9:30 AM 1:30 PM - 4:30 PM 8:30 PM - 11:30 PM 3:30 AM - 6:30 AM	10:30 AM - 1:30 PM 5:30 PM - 8:30 PM 12:30 AM - 3:30 AM	7:30 AM - 10:30 AM 2:30 PM - 5:30 PM 9:30 PM - 12:30 AM 4:30 AM - 7:30 AM	11:30 AM - 2:30 PM 6:30 PM - 9:30 PM 1:30 AM - 4:30 AM
7:00 AM - 10:00 AM 2:00 PM - 5:00 PM 9:00 PM - 12:00 AM 4:00 AM - 7:00 AM	11:00 AM - 2:00 PM 6:00 PM - 9:00 PM 1:00 AM - 4:00 AM	8:00 AM - 11:00 AM 3:00 PM - 6:00 PM 10:00 PM - 1:00 AM 5:00 AM - 8:00 AM	12:00 PM -3:00 PM 7:00 PM - 10:00 PM 2:00 AM - 5:00 AM
7:30 AM - 10:30 AM 2:30 AM - 5:30 PM 9:30 PM - 12:30 AM 4:30 AM - 7:30 AM	11:30 AM - 2:30 PM 6:30 PM - 9:30 PM 1:30 AM - 4:30 AM	8:30 AM - 11:30 AM 3:30 PM - 6:30 PM 10:30 PM - 1:30 AM 5:30 AM - 8:30 AM	12:30 PM -3:30 PM 7:30 PM - 10:30 PM 2:30 AM - 5:30 AM

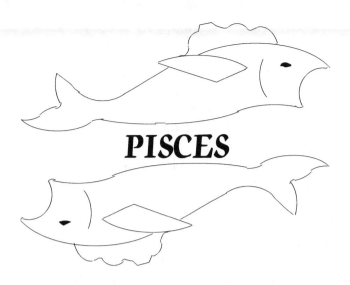

PISCES

There is no getting away from the fact, that there are only nine numbers by which all our calculations on this earth are made. Beyond these nine numbers, all the rest are repetition, as 10 is a 1 with a 0 added, eleven (11) 1+1=2; and so on. Every number, no matter how high, can be reduced to a single figure. This is why your lucky numbers first appear as single numbers, followed by numbers adding up to this single number, up to 31. However, any number over 31 which adds up to any of your single lucky numbers, is also lucky for you.

Your first lucky number is - 4 - and all numbers adding up to 4, such as 13-22-31 - Lucky day Sunday. This number was determined by combining your celestial number with other factors of your sun sign.

Your luckiest number is 4. Bear this in mind at all times. When you buy a ticket of any sort, make sure that the serial number has the predominant number 4 in it, and buy it during one of your lucky periods. Also a street address containing one or more 4's; horse number 4, player number 4 in a game; a 4 rolled in dice; room number 4 in a hotel/motel; and so on. These are all considered fortunate for you. You can also combine number 4 with your other lucky numbers.

Your second lucky number is your birth date.

Your third lucky number is - 3 - as well as 12-21-30 - Lucky day Thursday. This is the number assigned to the planet Jupiter, ruler of Pisces.

NOTE: Since number 3 is part of the 3-6-9 combination, you will have a certain degree of luck with 6-15-24 (lucky day Friday) and 9-18-27 (lucky day Tuesday). All these numbers are especially lucky on Tuesday, Thursday and Friday.

NOTE: Since the planet Neptune is co-ruler of Pisces, you could have a certain degree of luck with numbers 7-16-25 and 2-11-20-29 (lucky days, Monday and Sunday).

BIRTH DATES

NUMBERS: 1 - 10 - 19 - 28
LUCKY DAYS: Sunday and Monday

People born on one of these dates are fortunate, because these numbers are related to 4-13-22-31 (lucky day Sunday), and the series of 1 and 4 are interrelated to 2-11-20-29 and 7-16-25 (lucky day Monday). Therefore, all these numbers are especially lucky on Sunday and Monday.

Your lucky yearly periods are; July 20th to August 28th and March 21st to April 28th.

NUMBERS: 2 - 11 - 20 - 29
LUCKY DAYS: Monday and Sunday

People born on one of these dates are fortunate, because these numbers are related to 7-16-25 (lucky day Monday), and the series of 2 and 7 are interrelated to 1-10-19-28 and 4-13-22-31 (lucky day Sunday). Therefore, all these numbers are especially lucky on Monday and Sunday.

Your lucky yearly period is from June 21st to July 27th.

NUMBERS: 3 - 12 - 21 - 30
LUCKY DAY: Thursday

If one of these dates is your birth date, these numbers are extremely lucky for you, since they happen to be the same as your third lucky number.

NOTE: Since these numbers are part of the 3-6-9 combination, you will have a certain degree of luck with 6-15-24 (lucky day Friday) and 9-18-27 (lucky day Tuesday). All these numbers are especially lucky on Thursday, Tuesday and Friday.

Your lucky yearly periods are; February 19th to March 27th and November 21st to December 27th.

NUMBERS: 4 - 13 - 22 - 31
LUCKY DAYS: Sunday and Monday.

If one of these dates is your birth date, these numbers are extremely lucky for you, since they happen to be the same as your first lucky number.

People born on one of these dates are fortunate, because these numbers are related to 1-10-19-28 (lucky day Sunday), and the series of 4 and 1 are interrelated to 2-11-20-29 and 7-16-25 (lucky day Monday). Therefore, all these numbers are especially lucky on Sunday and Monday.

Your lucky yearly period is from June 21st to August 30th.

NUMBERS: 5 - 14 - 23
LUCKY DAY: Wednesday

You will also have a certain degree of luck on Fridays.

Your lucky yearly periods are; May 21st to June 27th and August 21st to September 27th.

NUMBERS: 6 - 15 - 24
LUCKY DAY: Friday

NOTE: Since these numbers are part of the 3-6-9 combination, you will have a certain degree of luck with 3-12-21-30 (lucky day Thursday) and 9-18-27 (lucky day Tuesday). All these numbers are especially lucky on Friday, Tuesday and Thursday.

Your lucky yearly periods are; April 20th to May 27th and September 21st to October 27th.

NUMBERS: 7 - 16 - 25

LUCKY DAYS: Monday and Sunday

People born on one of these dates are fortunate, because these numbers are related to 2-11-20-29 (lucky day Monday), and the series of 7 and 2 are interrelated to 1-10-19-28 and 4-13-22-31 (lucky day Sunday). Therefore, all these numbers are especially lucky on Monday and Sunday.

Your lucky yearly period is from June 21st to July 27th, and less strongly from this date to the end of August.

NUMBERS: 8 - 17 - 26

LUCKY DAY: Saturday

Since number 8 has a connection to number 4, you could have a certain degree of luck on Sundays.

Your lucky yearly periods are; from December 21st to December 31st, all of January up to February 26th.

NUMBERS: 9 - 18 - 27

LUCKY DAY: Tuesday

NOTE: Since these numbers are part of the 3-6-9 combination, you will have a certain degree of luck with 3-12-21-30 (lucky day Thursday) and 6-15-24 (lucky day Friday). All these numbers are especially lucky on Tuesday, Thursday and Friday.

Your lucky yearly periods are; March 21st to April 27th and October 21st to November 27th.

DECANS

Note: Decans are Stars or constellations that rise once every ten days and by which the ancient Egyptians used to tell time.

There are certain periods during the year that are most fortunate for you, when your chances of winning are amplified even more.

If you were born on February 20, 21, 22, 23, 24, 25, 26, 27, 28, 29 - the following periods are lucky for you.

April 21st to May 2nd

June 22nd to July 3rd
October 23rd to November 2nd
December 22nd to 31st

If you were born on March 1, 2, 3, 4, 5, 6, 7, 8, 9, 10 - the following periods are lucky for you.
January 1st to 10th
May 1st to 12th
July 2nd to 13th
November 1st to 12th

If you were born on March 11, 12, 13, 14, 15, 126, 17, 18, 19, 20 - the following periods are lucky for you.
January 10th to 20th
May 11th to 21st
July 13th to 23rd
November 11th to 22nd

The lucky periods in your Personal Luck Chart, and your lucky numbers, remain the same for the rest of your life. They are based on your birth date and the time of sunrise, which varies greatly throughout the year. I have provided you with sunrise times from 3:00 a.m. to 9:00 a.m.. Your lucky hours have been indicated for each hour of sunrise, for each day of the week. The only thing that changes is the time of sunrise, so all you have to do is check the sunrise time on any given day of the year, and go by the lucky hours listed for that time and day. For this reason, it doesn't matter if it's standard or daylight savings time. It also doesn't matter if you are at home or in another part of the world. Just go by the sunrise time for the location you are in, to determine your lucky hours.

Refer to *Sample Chart* on page *36* for instructions.

PISCES PERSONAL

SUNRISE	SUNDAY	MONDAY	TUESDAY
3:00 AM **to** **3:29 AM**	7:00 AM -10:00 AM 2:00 PM - 5:00 PM 9:00 PM - 12:00 AM	4:00 AM - 7:00 AM 11:00 AM - 2:00 PM 6:00 PM - 9:00 PM 1:00 AM - 4:00 AM	8:00 AM - 11:00 AM 3:00 PM - 6:00 PM 10:00 PM - 1:00 AM
3:30 AM **to** **3:59 AM**	7:30 AM -10:30 AM 2:30 PM - 5:30 PM 9:30 PM - 12:30 AM	4:30 AM - 7:30 AM 11:30 AM - 2:30 PM 6:30 PM - 9:30 PM 1:30 AM - 4:30 AM	8:30 AM - 11:30 AM 3:30 PM - 6:30 PM 10:30 PM - 1:30 AM
4:00 AM **to** **4:29 AM**	8:00 AM -11:00 AM 3:00 PM - 6:00 PM 10:00 PM - 1:00 AM	5:00 AM - 8:00 AM 12:00 PM - 3:00 PM 7:00 PM - 10:00 PM 2:00 AM - 5:00 AM	9:00 AM - 12:00 PM 4:00 PM - 7:00 PM 11:00 PM - 2:00 AM
4:30 AM **to** **4:59 AM**	8:30 AM -11:30 AM 3:30 PM - 6:30 PM 10:30 PM - 1:30 AM	5:30 AM - 8:30 AM 12:30 PM - 3:30 PM 7:30 PM - 10:30 PM 2:30 AM - 5:30 AM	9:30 AM - 12:30 PM 4:30 PM - 7:30 PM 11:30 PM - 2:30 AM
5:00 AM **to** **5:29 AM**	9:00 AM -12:00 PM 4:00 PM - 7:00 PM 11:00 PM - 2:00 AM	6:00 AM - 9:00 AM 1:00 PM - 4:00 PM 8:00 PM - 11:00 PM 3:00 AM - 6:00 AM	10:00 AM - 1:00 PM 5:00 PM - 8:00 PM 12:00 AM - 3:00 AM
5:30 AM **to** **5:59 AM**	9:30 AM -12:30 PM 4:30 PM - 7:30 PM 11:30 PM - 2:30 AM	6:30 AM - 9:30 AM 1:30 PM - 4:30 PM 8:30 PM - 11:30 PM 3:30 AM - 6:30 AM	10:30 AM - 1:30 PM 5:30 PM - 8:30 PM 12:30 AM - 3:30 AM

Refer to *Sample Chart* on page *36* for instructions.

LUCK CHART

WEDNESDAY	THURSDAY	FRIDAY	SATURDAY
5:00 AM - 8:00 AM 12:00 PM - 3:00 PM 7:00 PM - 10:00 PM	2:00 AM - 5:00 AM 9:00 AM - 12:00 PM 4:00 PM - 7:00 PM 11:00 PM - 2:00 AM	6:00 AM - 9:00 AM 1:00 PM - 4:00 PM 8:00 PM - 11:00 PM	3:00 AM - 6:00 AM 10:00 AM - 1:00 PM 5:00 PM - 8:00 PM 12:00 AM - 3:00 AM
5:30 AM - 8:30 AM 12:30 PM - 3:30 PM 7:30 PM - 10:30 PM	2:30 AM - 5:30 AM 9:30 AM - 12:30 PM 4:30 PM - 7:30 PM 11:30 PM - 2:30 AM	6:30 AM - 9:30 AM 1:30 PM - 4:30 PM 8:30 PM - 11:30 PM	3:30 AM - 6:30 AM 10:30 AM - 1:30 PM 5:30 PM - 8:30 PM 12:30 AM - 3:30 AM
6:00 AM - 9:00 AM 1:00 PM - 4:00 PM 8:00 PM - 11:00 PM	3:30 AM - 6:00 AM 10:00 AM - 1:00 PM 5:00 PM - 8:00 PM 12:00 AM - 3:00 AM	7:00 AM - 10:00 AM 2:00 PM - 5:00 PM 9:00 PM - 12:00 AM	4:00 AM - 7:00 AM 11:00 AM - 2:00 PM 6:00 PM - 9:00 PM 1:00 AM - 4:00 AM
6:30 AM - 9:30 AM 1:30 PM - 4:30 PM 8:30 PM - 11:30 PM	3:30 AM - 6:30 AM 10:30 AM - 1:30 PM 5:30 PM - 8:30 PM 12:30 AM - 3:30 AM	7:30 AM - 10:30 AM 2:30 PM - 5:30 PM 9:30 PM - 12:30 AM	4:30 AM - 7:30 AM 11:30 AM - 2:30 PM 6:30 PM - 9:30 PM 1:30 AM - 4:30 AM
7:00 AM - 10:00 AM 2:00 PM - 5:00 PM 9:00 PM - 12:00 AM	4:00 AM - 7:00 AM 11:00 AM - 2:00 PM 6:00 PM - 9:00 PM 1:00 AM - 4:00 AM	8:00 AM - 11:00 AM 3:00 PM - 6:00 PM 10:00 PM - 1:00 AM	5:00 AM - 8:00 AM 12:00 PM - 3:00 PM 7:00 PM - 10:00 PM 2:00 AM - 5:00 AM
7:30 AM - 10:30 AM 2:30 PM - 5:30 PM 9:30 PM - 12:30 AM	4:30 AM - 7:30 AM 11:30 AM - 2:30 PM 6:30 PM - 9:30 PM 1:30 AM - 4:30 AM	8:30 AM - 11:30 AM 3:30 PM - 6:30 PM 10:30 PM - 1:30 AM	5:30 AM - 8:30 AM 12:30 PM - 3:30 PM 7:30 PM - 10:30 PM 2:30 AM - 5:30 AM

SUNRISE	SUNDAY	MONDAY	TUESDAY
6:00 AM to **6:29 AM**	10:00 AM -1:00 PM 5:00 PM - 8:00 PM 12:00 AM - 3:00 AM	7:00 AM - 10:00 AM 2:00 PM - 5:00 PM 9:00 PM - 12:00 AM 4:00 AM - 7:00 AM	11:00 AM - 2:00 PM 6:00 PM - 9:00 PM 1:00 AM - 4:00 AM
6:30 AM to **6:59 AM**	10:30 AM -1:30 PM 5:30 PM - 8:30 PM 12:30 AM - 3:30 AM	7:30 AM - 10:30 AM 2:30 PM - 5:30 PM 9:30 PM - 12:30 AM 4:30 AM - 7:30 AM	11:30 AM - 2:30 PM 6:30 PM - 9:30 PM 1:30 AM - 4:30 AM
7:00 AM to **7:29 AM**	11:00 AM - 2:00 PM 6:00 PM - 9:00 PM 1:00 AM - 4:00 AM	8:00 AM - 11:00 AM 3:00 PM - 6:00 PM 10:00 PM - 1:00 AM 5:00 AM - 8:00 AM	5:00 AM - 8:00 AM 12:00 PM - 3:00 PM 7:00 PM - 10:00 PM 2:00 AM - 5:00 AM
7:30 AM to **7:59 AM**	11:30 AM - 2:30 PM 6:30 PM - 9:30 PM 1:30 AM - 4:30 AM	8:30 AM - 11:30 AM 3:30 PM - 6:30 PM 10:30 PM - 1:30 AM 5:30 AM - 8:30 AM	5:30 AM - 8:30 AM 12:30 PM - 3:30 PM 7:30 PM - 10:30 PM 2:30 AM - 5:30 AM
8:00 AM to **8:29 AM**	12:00 PM - 3:00 PM 7:00 PM - 10:00 PM 2:00 AM - 5:00 AM	9:00 AM - 12:00 PM 4:00 PM - 7:00 PM 11:00 PM - 2:00 AM	6:00 AM - 9:00 AM 1:00 PM - 4:00 PM 8:00 PM - 11:00 PM 3:00 AM - 6:00 AM
8:30 AM to **8:59 AM**	12:30 PM - 3:30 PM 7:30 PM - 10:30 PM 2:30 AM - 5:30 AM	9:30 AM - 12:30 PM 4:30 PM - 7:30 PM 11:30 PM - 2:30 AM	6:30 AM - 9:30 AM 1:30 PM - 4:30 PM 8:30 PM - 11:30 PM 3:30 AM - 6:30 AM

WEDNESDAY	THURSDAY	FRIDAY	SATURDAY
8:00 AM - 11:00 AM 3:00 PM - 6:00 PM 10:00 PM - 1:00 AM	5:00 AM - 8:00 AM 12:00 AM - 3:00 PM 7:00 PM - 10:00 PM 2:00 AM - 5:00 AM	9:00 AM - 12:00 PM 4:00 PM -7:00 PM 11:00 PM - 2:00 AM	6:00 AM -9:00 AM 1:00 PM - 4:00 PM 8:00 PM -11:00 PM 3:00 AM - 6:00 AM
8:30 AM - 11:30 AM 3:30 PM - 6:30 PM 10:30 PM - 1:30 AM	5:30 AM - 8:30 AM 12:30 PM - 3:30 PM 7:30 PM - 10:30 PM 2:30 AM - 5:30 AM	9:30 AM - 12:30 PM 4:30 PM - 7:30 PM 11:30 PM - 2:30 AM	6:30 AM - 9:30 AM 1:30 PM - 4:30 PM 8:30 PM - 11:30 PM 3:30 AM - 6:30 AM
9:00 AM - 12:00 PM 4:00 PM - 7:00 PM 11:00 PM - 2:00 AM	6:00 AM - 9:00 AM 1:00 PM - 4:00 PM 8:00 PM - 11:00 PM 3:00 AM - 6:00 AM	10:00 AM - 1:00 PM 5:00 PM - 8:00 PM 12:00 AM - 3:00 AM	7:00 AM - 10:00 AM 2:00 PM - 5:00 PM 9:00 PM - 12:00 AM 4:00 AM - 7:00 AM
9:30 AM - 12:30 AM 4:30 PM - 7:30 PM 11:30 PM - 2:30 AM	6:30 AM - 9:30 AM 1:30 PM - 4:30 PM 8:30 PM - 11:30 PM 3:30 AM - 6:30 AM	10:30 AM - 1:30 PM 5:30 PM - 8:30 PM 12:30 AM - 3:30 AM	7:30 AM - 10:30 AM 2:30 PM - 5:30 PM 9:30 PM - 12:30 AM 4:30 AM - 7:30 AM
10:00 AM - 1:00 PM 5:00 PM - 8:00 PM 12:00 AM - 3:00 AM	7:00 AM - 10:00 AM 2:00 PM - 5:00 PM 9:00 PM - 12:00 AM 4:00 AM - 7:00 AM	11:00 AM - 2:00 PM 6:00 PM - 9:00 PM 1:00 AM - 4:00 AM	8:00 AM - 11:00 AM 3:00 PM - 6:00 PM 10:00 PM - 1:00 AM 5:00 AM - 8:00 AM
10:30 AM - 1:30 PM 5:30 PM - 8:30 PM 12:30 AM - 3:30 AM	7:30 AM - 10:30 AM 2:30 AM - 5:30 PM 9:30 PM - 12:30 AM 4:30 AM - 7:30 AM	11:30 AM - 2:30 PM 6:30 PM - 9:30 PM 1:30 AM - 4:30 AM	8:30 AM - 11:30 AM 3:30 PM - 6:30 PM 10:30 PM - 1:30 AM 5:30 AM - 8:30 AM

I have been writing poetry as a hobby most of my life. Many years ago, during a period when I was experiencing many difficulties, I decided to write a poem that I could recite every morning, to help me start my day off right. It made a big difference, and I believe it brought me more luck in all my endeavors. I call it my "good luck" poem. Published 1996 in the anthology "Daybreak on the Land," by the National Library of Poetry, in Owing Mills, MD.

GOOD MORNING LORD

Good morning Lord!
I'm beginning a new day
Please come along to guide me
And protect me come what may

Talk to me Lord!
I want to hear your wisdom
Then it's mostly up to me
You have given me much freedom

Walk with me Lord!
Pick me up should I stumble
Just give me a little nudge
If I complain and grumble

You're my friend Lord!
Whatever happens You're there
You love me for what I am
Always showing that You care

I need you Lord!
Take my hand and lead the way
Together there is no limit
Let us both have a great day

Claire Doyle-Beland

Claire Doyle Beland was born in Sudbury, Ontario, Canada, where she still resides close to her family. She has done some professional singing, especially during her younger years, and has also won some poetry awards. For over twenty-five years, she has studied astrology and numerology, and has found these sciences very enlightening and fascinating. She would be interested in hearing from anyone who experiences exceptional luck, using their lucky numbers, lucky days, or lucky periods.

She would like to acknowledge that some of her information or ideas can be found in other source books. In particular: CHEIRO BOOK OF NUMBERS - by Cheiro. Published by Prentice Hall Press in 1988. ZOLAR'S BOOK OF ASTROLOGY, DREAMS, NUMBERS AND LUCKY DAYS - by Zolar. Published by Prentice Hall Press in 1990.

If you wish to correspond with Claire about this book, please forward all correspondence to:

Ozark Mountain Publishing
P.O. Box 754, Huntsville, AR 72740
Attn: Claire Doyle-Beland
E-mail - www.ozarkmt.com

Other Books Published
by
Ozark Mountain Publishing

Conversations with Nostradamus Volume I........ by Dolores Cannon
Conversations with Nostradamus Volume II....... by Dolores Cannon
Conversations with Nostradamus Volume III..... by Dolores Cannon
Jesus and the Essenes............................. by Dolores Cannon
They Walked with Jesus........................... by Dolores Cannon
Between Death and Life........................... by Dolores Cannon
(Formerly titled Conversations with a Spirit)
A Soul Remembers Hiroshima .... by Dolores Cannon
Keepers of the Garden............................. by Dolores Cannon
The Legend of Starcrash........................... by Dolores Cannon
Legacy from the Stars............................. by Dolores Cannon
The Custodians.................................... by Dolores Cannon
Beauty and the Priest..................... by Reverend Patrick McNamara
I Have Lived Before........................... by Sture Lönnerstrand
The Forgotten Woman........................... by Arun & Sunanda Gandhi

-Books Soon to be Released -

Mankind - Child of the Stars .... by Max H. Flindt & Otto O. Binder
Gandhi - The Essential Writings .... by Arun Gandhi
The Convoluted Universe .... by Dolores Cannon

For more information about any of the above titles, or other
titles in our catalog, write or visit our web site.

P.O. Box 332
West Fork, AR 72774
WWW.OZARKMT.COM
1-800-935-0045 / 1-800-230-0312

Wholesale Inquiries Welcome